WEATHERING IT

To Elej.

Best wishes
Xmas 87
in purdy's
nearly
class 7.

Douglas LePan seated in front of a drawing of himself made by
Wyndham Lewis in 1941. (Robert Lansdale Photography)

Douglas LePan

Weathering It

Complete Poems
1948–1987

Canadian Cataloguing in Publication Data

LePan, Douglas, 1914-
Weathering it

(The Modern Canadian poets)
Poems.
Includes index.
ISBN 0-7710-5267-7

I. Title.   II. Series.

PS8523.E62W42 1987   C811'.54   C87-094322-7
PR9199.2.L45W42 1987

The publisher makes grateful acknowledgment to the Canada Council and
the Ontario Arts Council for their financial assistance.

Set in Caslon by The Typeworks, Vancouver

Printed and bound in Canada

McClelland and Stewart
The Canadian Publishers
481 University Avenue
Toronto, Ontario
M5G 2E9

CONTENTS

Weathering It (1987)

The Wounded Prince (1948)

WEATHERING IT

I

LIKE A BATTLEFIELD

Waking in the very early morning, with memories
trampling like armies through the mist, his whole life
unrolls before him in the pale gun-metal light,
disposing itself round hummocks of innocent childhood,
of boyhood, of green adolescence, of manhood, and now
of this accurst old age, the years lumbering by like gun-limbers
but so indistinctly that he can hardly tell infantry
from artillery, or victory from defeat. So what does it come to?
Once he would have gloried in the eagles dazzling above
the mist and in an Emperor of unclouded victories.
But now? Now he can only find comfort with Kutúzov,
that drowsy genius of defeat, old, one-eyed, sabre-
scarred, yet able from weakness and inevitable withdrawal
to wheedle ambiguous triumph like a long winter's tale.

II

Auburn hair with curls uncut. As soon as he could walk
and long before he could read, he would climb upstairs
to a small attic room where piles of magazines were stacked,
with pictures of battles in the First World War — the dead
and wounded, the casualty clearing stations, the field hospitals,
dead uhlans, dead tommies, dead *poilus,* at Mons, Ypres,
the Marne (although he didn't know any of those names yet) —
and pore fascinated over the pictures hour after hour.
Brown eyes under curls uncut — they were drinking it in,
that subtlest, far-fetched venom, becoming infected
with the history that his choice of a birthday had committed him to.
And, strange, that is his earliest memory of his earliest home,
in that lost innocent house of his first imaginings,
in the bosom of "Toronto the Good," of "the City of Churches."

III

THE LIFE OF CAMPS: NIAGARA-ON-THE-LAKE

The skies scored and scissored with flags and bugle-calls,
and now and then band-music drifting down to the river —
it comes floating back to him as if from a long-closed album,
that and the dust kicked up by hundreds of army boots
(it prickles his eyes and his nostrils) as he watches the parade
pass by the reviewing-stand on a hot summer afternoon,
a small boy in a sailor-suit on the fringe of the quarrels
of Mittel-Europa. In the evenings his mother reads
him and his brother to sleep with stories of Peter Rabbit
and Little Mrs. Tittlemouse. In the mornings he goes on walks
with his father's batman to a deserted fort by the river.
And suddenly he feels a shy tenderness for the small boy
(so long forgotten!) in a sailor-suit. For who could have told him
he had been born into the most brutal age since the world began?

IV

A LONG REMISSION

Then there was a long remission. His mother and father
stood over him like shade trees, like elms or maples, on a leafy
street in the Annex in Toronto, protecting him, shielding him,
as though history didn't exist, or had been put out to pasture,
and he could grow up unafraid of the circling seasons.
In spring, picking dandelions on the way home from school
and being caressed by all the green in the warm green grass
and in the unfolding leaves that reached up to the turrets of a rich
man's folly; dawdling on into the summer holidays
(but that's another story); on into the flagrancy of autumn
flowers, a blazing cauldron of red and gold, pierced
by the glint of coming frost and poignant with the cries
of children playing. As he looks back, the leaves are gala.
A red-gold street. Leaves drizzling on a punted football.

V

WINTER DAY, TORONTO

City of vapours! Vapours from mouths and nostrils,
from stacks and chimneys, from the city's steaming entrails,
all turned by the blazing, blistering cold (it's ten
below) into pale crystal signatures of life and breath,
the whole city vapouring in the freezing morning air
like a great hibernating animal, just breathing, gasping;
and boys in snow-packs crunching the packed hard snow;
and little sprigs with scarves tied tight across their mouths;
and sleighs, with sleigh-bells, delivering milk and groceries
(it's in nineteen-twenty-two, not 'eighty-two, this snow-scape)
to a house on Walmer Road where, behind storm-windows,
evening will bring music and laughter rising in bright
arpeggios, higher and higher, like the pink and gold
in the warm sunlight of a great Bonnard or Vuillard.

VI

GEORGIAN BAY

Summers were less a season than an utter transfiguration,
an escape for a city boy into the splendour of wind blowing,
almost always blowing (and almost always from the west),
into another age, another more lustrous dispensation, with
        everything
more vivid, the water vivid blue, the pine trees vivid green,
the stars the colours of the spectrum in the pitch-black sky,
and everything bathed in timelessness. In the wind
his nerves and muscles are laced into a sun-burnt miracle
defiant of dualisms – yet still open towards transcendence –
a slim knot, a slight thickening of being into consciousness.
On the waves the sun is playing brilliant toccatas. The clouds
are scored for a descant of flutes. Down swoops a tern for fish
and soars up again. He feels himself transformed, uplifted,
held in the wild soaring beak of a transcendent perfection.

VII

ISLANDS OF SUMMER

Since they have gone from him, years ago, into the lap
of the rich who can buy anything (a young boy's innocence,
an old man's longing), he has to imagine them, the islands
of summer. A few acres of pines and cedars where he knew
almost every tree. Abrupt granite rising from the clearest
water in all the world. Crowned with a tangled diadem
of blue green foliage, with proud cedar-waxwings nesting there.
A secluded thicket where you could lie all afternoon, listening
to the warblers. And always beneath birdsong the sound of water.
Tonight he is imagining the calm after a three-day blow,
the roar of the open from the swell on the outer reefs,
while here on the inner islands the waves are gently lapping,
and gently rocking the launch that's tied to the dock. As he glides
into sleep, he even dreams he can hear the tiller-ropes rustling.

VIII

SWIMMING AT NIGHT, POINTE-AU-BARIL

One moment of Descartes. A hurricane lamp on the dock,
paddles, the sleek red skin of a canvas canoe,
a diver naked between black sky black water,
his mind eyeing the lamp, the paddles, the canoe,
and eyeing himself as he eyes them and then in the instant
he is over the still dark mirror — reflected there —
eyeing his body too, his mind and his body
now immaculately separate in Cartesian distinction.
Then Descartes refuted. The water engulfing distinctions,
distinctions between mind and body, mind and matter,
subject and object, the self and the ineffable not-self,
the water claiming its child again as its own,
while the sweet hiss of the bubbles the swimmer makes
kisses away Descartes to a fare-thee-well.

IX

A FULL MOON IN AUGUST

Sometimes the shards of moonlight in the city are enough
to waft him back. To a full moon glittering on the water,
the islands still and silvered, criss-crossed by amethyst
shadows, as a youth emerges from them on to bare rock
and stands there tranced, transfixed — a native Endymion
in a khaki shirt, drinking in the overflowing splendour,
drinking it in, breathing it in, and thinking (if he thinks at all)
only of the rhythms that bind him to the rest of nature,
until — abandoning all thought, all bonds, all breath —
he rises on this glittering romanza of linked silver notes
into the arms of a bright swoon of everlastingness . . .
Then descending slowly. Mortality returning. The moon
will set. What's left are only shards and glimmerings down
the decades. A far estuary! Confluence of love, light, and memory!

X

ARTHURIAN ENCHANTMENTS

So, he had his own standards of splendour, and some few inklings
as a poet. But what of the prime stuff of poetry – words?
Start with a boy engrossed in "King Arthur and his Knights"
and let that sink in until he is hardly aware of the residue
lost in his bloodstream. Now he has left knights in armour far
behind, their crests, plumes, mantlings, streaming in the wind;
but he still likes a style of military dash and crispness,
with hints of heraldry, of tapestry, of ancient music.
He agrees with Nabokov that "The enchantment is everything,"
although he has almost forgotten Merlin and Morgana le Fay.
But even now is he sufficiently wary of chivalric adventures
undertaken for the flimsiest of reasons – or for no reason at all –
adventures that lead deeper and deeper into the romantic wood?
Even now does he realize that those wounds were sometimes
        for real?

XI

LEARNING GREEK

See him at the blackboard, among all those pothooks, vain
as a little peacock, because he is studying a subject that not
many boys take. And then, not much later, memorizing
long strings of Greek words in his bedroom at home, pacing
up and down after he's finished the rest of his homework.
And then, still later, able to distinguish neatly the uses
of the various cases (dative of instrument, of manner, etc. . . .)
and pinpoint them triumphantly for you there in the margin.
Insufferable? Yes, perhaps — except it was all fairly innocent.
And a haunting summons is sounding beyond the
        vaingloriousness,
flute-music in the far distance of a style of naked purity,
the style of Sappho and Simonides, and a far summons, too,
towards such a habit of life, frank, candid, unashamed,
like a sky-blue lake that glitters beyond a screen of birch trees.

XII

FROM THE *SYMPOSIUM*

It was almost laughable what they served up to him first
— but blessings on them just the same! From the *Symposium*
what they chose was the passage about Socrates as a foot-soldier,
as a hoplite at Potidaea and Delium, and a formidable one too,
about his courage, his oddity, his endurance of hardships.
(It was only much later — and on his own! — that he learned
about Alcibiades making a pass at him.) Interesting, and a good
preparation perhaps for what was to come, when he concluded
that one war is more like any other than it resembles what
appears in the newspapers; still, pretty dull fare for a boy
who was dreaming rather of Aphrodite rising from the foam
and of the athletes at Olympia sleek from oil and the strigil.
But then, as so often, the needs of his imagination came in second
to that other, more powerful, necessity, the course of history.

READING THE *ILIAD*

The one thing certain is that we're all going down to defeat.
You can't win. Death, even a quiet death, will see to that.
Reading the *Iliad* week after week with a wise master
who would insist that Achilles was "born to so short a life"
and that Hector knew that "sacred Ilium must perish," a master
who had heard of no dispensation that could change that lot,
who accepted it, welcomed it, rejoiced in it, but believed
that it still mattered enormously to try to make something of it
and that all ages could be, should be, heroic ages —
ah, there was something to stick to your ribs, hard-tack
to keep in your knapsack for whatever event might come.
The marble face of the blind old rhapsode of Chios
fades into the face of that long-dead master of his youth,
a weathered urn whose tears had all been turned into wine.

XIV

AN ARTICLE OF FAITH

What was he like, then, as a boy growing up? A prig?
I'm afraid so, although never a milksop. A shy, bright butterfingers
who could always be trusted to drop any ball that came
his way, but who always stood head of the class, and, worse,
wanted to, needed to, and would go to any lengths to see
that he did. Yet older boys would come to him for his advice
about their lives or their love-affairs — he didn't have any —
and would follow it, too. He knew there was an anomaly
                 somewhere
in his nervous system. (A doctor confirmed that only yesterday.)
But he knew there was inordinate strength somewhere, too,
and that the strength was somehow mixed with the weakness,
flowed from it, or flowed from the same source. And so to this day
he still holds it as an article of faith that to be wounded is
to be human; and that to be human is to be wounded. Selah!

XV

A MARCH DAY

A kingbird battling with a hawk, and light swaying
and wavering — cloud and then sun and tumbling cloud
again — as he walks through a land of equinox,
of unease and melting snow, wondering what it all
comes to and how it all happened. Then the light shifts . . .
It was on a day like this (he had been reading Spenser and had
sauntered out for a walk) that he made his decision:
in spite of every weakness, every infirmity, to take
all the hurdles. Of public life, private life, peace, war,
the whole issue. Heroism or folly? He still doesn't know.
But he knows that, although he couldn't foretell the outcome
(it was the making of him and his undoing), it was done
with his eyes open, it was a choice that came from the core
of his being. He chose. And he read no more that day.

XVI

RATTLESNAKES IN A BARREL

Like a lighthouse beam, it was a knowledge that came and went,
knowledge of how contradictory he was, once he admitted —
at long last! — the rights of the usurper lurking between
his legs and so released a great prince from prison.
The play of light and shade became sharper, the chiaroscuro
deeper, as he was called with terror and delight into a scene
where the night sky's blue knife-edge and the shine of the gutter
were both whetted on the palate of longing, and envenomed.
The year Toronto was founded, when Mrs. Simcoe wanted
to see a rattlesnake, they brought her two of them in a barrel.
Now he was a nest of rattlers, a whole barrelful of them,
hissing voluptuously, dangerously together, although it was
seldom that he dared to look in and observe them. He knew,
          though.
And he knew that his days as a precocious schoolboy were over.

XVII

LOOKING BACK AT THE THIRTIES

Caught up in the claws of an evil time, the sky darkening,
cloud after cloud, black clouds and wings, and his brains
exposed to the sweep and the storm, every fold and furrow
crackling with messages coming in *en clair* from the far
corners of the earth, how could he settle to contemplation
or to some sweetness of words, or hope to set his contradictions
in order? The remission was over. And no one was innocent.
But could that be an excuse for inaction, as some casuists
were saying? It was an evil time for his coming of age,
and part of his coming of age was accepting necessity,
the pitiless necessity of a world of impossible choices,
that ordained that the necessary act could never be innocent.
But there lay his only way out towards some measure of freedom —
to take service and shelter under those black circling wings.

XVIII

FAR FROM HARVARD YARD

Nothing will do for this but fact, brute fact.
(Even Wallace Stevens, that suave fabulist of the inane,
knew that consciousness of war is "consciousness of fact.")
So — the fact that Tim Willcox was killed on Omaha Beach
on the 6th of June; that David Kelleher was killed at Iwo
Jima with the Marines; that Bill Fetcher went down with
the *Juneau* off Guadalcanal. His students all of them
and all of them friends, only a few years younger than he was:
Tim with his patrician temper and his stunning "summa";
David, everything that was best of the Boston Irish;
Bill with his taste for bow-ties and his love of Brahms.
Perhaps Bill most of all, questing, and fixed, and true!
As salt-water comes flooding down the companion-way
it still sluices away the eyes of an old man, weeping.

XIX

A HEAD FOUND AT BENEVENTUM

Begin with the likeness of a young man's head on a coin,
as if he were perhaps the Antinous beloved by Hadrian,
and let that grow into a bronze head, more strongly and subtly
modelled, the eyes deep set and heavy lidded, looking
either inward or out toward some unknowable future,
a little like the bronze head found at Beneventum
and now in the Louvre. And then bring all that to life
in the figure of a young American with the gentlest eyes
in all the world, a fine oarsman, but deep into Proust,
Joyce and Mann, always *disponible,* always open
to what the world had to offer, but always reserved,
always sure — a little too sure — of his own innocence.
The hooks went in very quietly. As no doubt they did
when Hadrian lost his heart and his head to Antinous.

XX

A NIGHTPIECE, OF LONDON IN THE BLACKOUT

A wash of greatcoats circling about the foot of Eros
dethroned. Of nameless and almost faceless figures in the dusk,
drawn from a dozen countries, but all homeless, solitary,
adrift, uneasily on leave for a few brief hours or days
from history and its iron formations — or else deserters from them.
And a sombre sky, that's careless of the heart's elections
but carelessly forgiving of every anonymous encounter,
a sky quivering to a subtext hidden beneath the greatcoats,
tissues and textures throbbing with their own imperatives
(which might be gross or pure, promiscuous or crazed with love,
or both), with a thousand different objects and inflections,
that yet transmit a single impulse to the indulgent air,
a deep pulse of loneliness and outright lust and longing —
to share their nakedness with someone. Now! Tonight!

XXI

TWO VIEWS OF ARMY HEADQUARTERS

It was like a Renaissance palace, he would tell his London
friends. And by that he meant that its corridors and conference-
rooms, even its gables and clustered chimneys, were informed
by the presence and virtue of a single man, as they might
have been by the presence of the prince at Urbino or Ferrara;
that his authority invested it; that its secrets were made darker,
its decisions more final because of his passionate intelligence.
The General (whom he was so proud to serve, who bore on his
        shoulders,
not only crossed swords and crowns, but life-and-death
        responsibility
for victory and certain loss) gave it his impress, coloured it,
from its sentries and clerks to its brigadiers, from its cellars
to the top of its parapets. At the time all that made it magical.
But now, compared with what followed, it seems rather flimsier,
more like a castle that a child might have cut out of paper.

XXII

CAMPAIGNING WEATHER

A tunic hanging in a closet... a dome blue with eternity...
a face glimpsed in battle, frightened, passionate, resolved...
these quicken, and will quicken till the day he dies, all
the artillery positions from Cassino to the gates of Rome,
when they moved almost every day, and every day was taut
and blue and lustrous as the last, and every day jewelled
with the danger of death. Death close as a comrade, moving
as they moved. From that first position, with the guns
          camouflaged
among the olive trees. There at eleven o'clock on a mild
May night the trees were cut through and a thousand guns
opened up, scaling the dark ramparts of heaven with licks
and ladders of flame. Coming out of the command-post, he
          remembers,
there was lodged in his brain a fragment both brutal and lyrical:
the birds thought the gun-fire was morning, and had started to
          sing.

XXIII

BELOW MONTE CASSINO

Having had too much sex the night before for a man
over sixty, he feels a dull ache in the small of his back
about the size of a pie-plate, and suddenly remembers
(as he urinates into the toilet-bowl) dead
American boys in a field below Monte Cassino
and how surprised he had been as he picked his way
forward (avoiding the bodies as best as he could,
scared shitless of trip-mines and shoe-mines and glass-mines)
by one dead boy lying face down in the mud
with his arms and his legs flung wide and one big wound
in the small of his back about the size of a pie-plate,
having been caught there by a fragment of mortar-fire —
surprised then, and still surprised now, that what was
oozing from the wide wound was, not blood, but shit.

XXIV

ON THE ROAD TO ROME

"Good luck, guns!" As clear as though it were yesterday
that voice comes to him in the middle of the night
as he stirs restlessly, trying to fall asleep again;
and he recognizes a stretch of the road to Rome (it must
have been somewhere between Aquino and Frosinone),
where the highway was suddenly littered with shattered
branches, and two files of riflemen had paused for a moment;
and he had paused, too, to get news from the infantry
and share a cigarette with a cheery kid from Toronto.
Then they had to move off. (They dabble in the hell-broth:
the artillery are licensed to sup from a longer spoon.)
But why is that boy's face tonight still plain as day
and his voice still deathly clear, as he calls out good-bye?
Why is it that tears are so suddenly wet on the pillow?

THE HAYSTACK

It doesn't take a Hiroshima to burn a man to a crisp.
A haystack will do. And what could be more bucolic
than that? And you get tired of sleeping in cellars or slit-trenches,
so why not behind a haystack that has simmered all day
in the warmth of an Italian September sun? But at night
the jackals are ready to spring, the German eighty-eights,
with their high muzzle-velocities and their low trajectories,
so that the haystack ignites like a torch and a gunner is burnt
to a crisp. How far back was that? thirty years? forty years?
He doesn't remember. He only remembers the stench
of fear, his own fear, and a grey army blanket, and a young
sunburned back alive on the banks of the Volturno,
then burning, burning. By dire subtleties such as these
he was being prepared for the carbonization of cities.

XXVI

PINK OLEANDERS

A split-second exposure. Arriving at the new command-post
to find that the one tree in the courtyard was splashed with blood
from the crotch to the next branch up, and the wall splattered
with pieces of charred flesh (looking like steak that had been left
too long on the grill), while a dog was slavering over other
morsels of charred flesh on the walk by the pink oleanders.
That was all that was left of the survey-officer and his driver,
both blown sky-high by a mine as they drove in the gate.
But no one cried out. They all had their jobs to do
and went about them quietly, hardly speaking in more than a
          whisper.
And he has had his own job to do, year after year.
Yet an exposure like that can colour a mind for a lifetime.
It helps to explain his view of the world. It helps, too,
to explain his distaste for those who are enchanted by violence.

XXVII

RIMINI: THE TEMPIO MALATESTIANO

An artilleryman should be able to draw you a panorama.
But the rose and purple clouds flowering out of
the vase of the roofless temple, and the ceaseless traffic —
guns, jeeps, transports, tanks and tank transporters —
flowing one way over a Bailey-bridge and the other way
over the stone bridge built by the Emperor Tiberius,
past floral confusions of corps and divisional signs,
on through the ruined city and out to a new campaign —
these all fail to compose into a sunset battle-piece,
as he looks up from the pages of Pound's Malatesta Cantos,
his mind wandering, looking for coherence somewhere,
anxious to throw off the taint of Rimini's vicious Lord,
anxious to find some solace for the restless dead,
but finding only a whole civilization with the roof blown off.

XXVIII

ALIVE, ALIVE-O

The song brings it back. (It was not all fear and disgust.)
The deep chiaroscuro of a farmhouse near Ravenna,
its roof stretched coracle-thin in the wash of shell-fire
overhead, as fragile as the telephone-lines to the batteries
(that he has just been out helping the line-crew to mend).
And he stands on his bunk in his long winter-underwear
as Sandy starts up on his wheeze-box. He picks up the tune
"with his coat so gay," tentatively first, then louder
and louder, "D'ye ken John Peel when he's far, far away?"
with his bare feet beating it out, stomping it out.
And then, all his cells beating and flashing like cymbals,
the sparks flying higher and higher, the roof wheezing outward,
on to "Dublin's fair city where girls are so pretty,"
belting it out now in crescendo, "alive, alive-o!"

XXIX

ICON ON A SULLEN GROUND

It was first in the Romagna (where Dante imagined Hell)
that he slipped through boredom into disgust, slipped almost into
despair. The mud. The cold. The seemingly endless
succession of infernal fosses and river-courses,
that led, so they claimed, to the valley of the Po, but instead
seemed only to lead to more casualties — and pointlessness.
As his gorge rose, he took to smoking one cigarette after
another (until he was wolfing down three packs a day)
to quiet his frazzled nerves that had been rubbed raw
by fields pitted and pock-marked by shell-fire, mortar-fire.
With the shrapnel whistling every which way, a signalman
comes running, then suddenly drops as though he had been hit;
but no! he squats there bare-assed to the wind, crippled with
dysentery — as a rude image of heroism in a field of fire.

XXX

THE DESPATCH CASE

The red morocco despatch-case with its gold-stamped
cypher (and its sheen caught from the tarnished mirrors and
chipped porcelain urns in superannuated palaces)
is far from being the only memento and residue
of his years as a diplomat. Paper. The torrents of paper,
that is what he remembers as much as anything else,
the despatches, the telegrams, the endless memoranda.
And the endless meetings. Words. Words. Words.
And behind it all occasionally a glimmer of hope
(as often as not frustrated), but mostly misery —
the Jews from the death-camps, the Palestinians evicted —
the clammy mist that rises from impossible choices.
Across his desk the sludge and sewage of a ravaged
world. He felt tired. He needed to wash his hands.

XXXI

SUNDAY AFTERNOONS

Yes, there were champagne cocktails one long hot Sunday
afternoon on the terrace of a villa overlooking Versailles
and conversation that was sometimes outrageous, but deft and
        allusive,
moving from persiflage to seriousness and then back again,
Jamesian almost in its fashionable nuance but spiked
with a frank lubricity that was far from Jamesian. But that
didn't happen often. (It happened only once, in fact.)
Most Sundays, and Saturdays, and other days, he would be
at his desk working on despatches and policy-papers
in aid, so he hoped, of the ordinary joes he had known
in the regiment — and all others like them — who were just
as complicated as any of the company drinking champagne,
just as shot through with delicate longings and contradictions,
but who couldn't have cared less for the Princesse de Polignac.

XXXII

SALLE DES PAS PERDUS

A memory of the peace conference flashes like laser-light
on the links in the chain between war and peace and war again —
the Soviet delegate delivering a statement as brusque and staccato
as the machine-guns set up in the cellar at Ekaterinburg,
while he is taking a breather in the room next door, an ante-room
arranged for coffee and cognac and conversation, a kind
of *salle des pas perdus*, he hears someone say. And with that
one phrase, he picks up the tread of a soldier on sentry-go,
the soft tread of a ghostly sentry pacing back and forth,
sent as their observer by the restless dead on every
side, whose wounds stain the draft articles of the peace treaties
and spread, and spread, till a wash of blood sweeps
over the Palais Luxembourg and all the innocent children
playing in its gardens. Is there no end to it? no end to it?

XXXIII

HIS YEARS IN WASHINGTON

"It's strange, I seldom think of my years in Washington,"
he will sometimes confess to his friends, with a little surprise,
strange that all those first-person notes, and third-person notes,
and *aide-mémoires*, and all those discussions at the State
     Department
over imports of fish-sticks, and lead and zinc, and rye and barley
(and all those dry martinis and old-fashioneds) should leave
so little impression, a few memories of Dean Acheson and Dulles
and Duncan Phillips, and that's about it. The imperial façades
and the monumental vistas have all melted into domesticity —
he was happily married by then, with two little boys —
and that's what he thinks of most, his wife and his sons,
hardly even remembering that this was the city where Lincoln
wrote the Second Inaugural and where Walt Whitman (who more
and more has become one of his heroes) tended the wounded.

XXXIV

A MARRIAGE EXEQUY, OR HOW IT SEEMS NOW

He dreams he is struggling to get free from his wife, and his wife's
house, where there's no room for him, or his clothes, or his books,
but from which he can't escape, even though he keeps telling her
that they're separated and have been for years now, yes, separated.
But she doesn't listen and still goes about whatever she's doing,
cooking, or painting, or rearranging the furniture *her* way
and pushing him more and more into a corner, until he's ready
to scream. Finally he struggles awake, and is relieved
to find that he's on his own, in his own flat, free of her.
"Relief," that's the first word to sound in the marriage exequy.
Then after that put "resentment," resentment at being left
and extruded. And after that "failure." A tangle of bitterness
almost completely concealing how happy he could be at first —
thick underbrush covering where wildflowers grew in the spring.

XXXV

DRIVING SOUTH, OR HOW IT SEEMED THEN

Into a new country, a new climate, warm with blossoms,
with bracts of the flowering dogwood floating in the woods,
deeper and deeper, past almond and flowering Judas
into the Carolinas of content and glimmering limbs.
The air is heavy with pollen and honeysuckle blooming,
so heavy it gets in their eyes, the scent and the pollen,
till they hardly know, either of them, who they are, or where,
entering a gold haze, a land where the enchanter of cups
and wands can weave spells both for darkness and broad day.
Open to love now are the intricacies of her magnolia thighs,
sword is fitted to scabbard. Then they lie panting on a cloth
of gold, still hardly themselves, tied to all favourable
signs of the zodiac, learning a whole new cosmology,
as a pale moon blossoming pours down on them epithalamium.

XXXVI

THALAMUS, OR AN INQUIRY WITH A FEW QUOTATIONS

Between "marriage as a cosmological experience" and "marriage
as an impossible contract" is there room for a little humanity?
So he ponders, as he considers the wreck of his own marriage
and the wreck of so many other marriages he can think of.
They speak nowadays of "no-fault marriage breakdown."
But of course in his case there were faults, plenty of them,
plenty of them on her side, and perhaps even more on his.
Did she enter into his problems? Hardly. But how far
did he enter into hers, into her anxieties and complexities,
or seek to consummate on the brain's vestal bridal-bed
a marriage that would be both a physical and an "intellectual
        thing"?
Well, that was a long while ago, he at last breaks off,
tired of this tedious inquisition. And he swears he must
have done something right; for there stand his two strong sons.

XXXVII

HIS SON SLEEPING

When the clouds lift, there are sometimes beautiful blue patches.
He can still see his firstborn son as he lies on his cot,
with one hand to his mouth as though blowing a trumpet
and the other thrown back in the slipstream, snug, fast asleep,
under the sky-blue coverlet that his mother made for him.
He might be a cherub majestically riding the storm,
as though on some astral errand, bringing space with him,
star-clusters, nebulae, galactic distance, till his father
(who has learned how desperate a place the world can be,
how shelterless) at first feels fear clamp round his heart
like ice-crystals. But then fear and distance are melted by
the streams from that milky breath and brow. And he bends
down to bless the whole dark universe for so precious a pledge,
for his son, in the blue of the night-light, so quietly sleeping.

XXXVIII

A BLOSSOMING TREE

"Is there anything finer than a blossoming tree?" That piping
voice comes from his little boy, who is now two or three,
as they stand looking out at the pink and white blossoms
of an apple tree, that is now in their backyard afloat.
And his father, heavy in his own thoughts, at first says nothing.
But then, brightening, lightening, this time says, "Nothing."
For what could be finer than a blossoming tree? Unless
conceivably (as once Mozart wrote) a scarlet coat,
or the white sail of a sailboat, or *"Voi che sapete,"* note
for note from a perfectly pitched and timbred throat.
Or a bright-eyed, blue-eyed boy, who is now two or three,
with a brow as broad as in Mozart's Verona portrait,
looking out at the apple tree afloat and glancing back
to ask, "Is there anything finer than a blossoming tree?"

XXXIX

A CONVERSATION PIECE

Standing at a party recently with his two grown sons,
he is struck, as he has been before, by subtle complicities.
Of course there are differences. His strength is made out of
      weakness
— is that anything to be ashamed of? — while theirs is made
out of strength, strength that perhaps came from their mother.
But the similarities are at least as important as the differences.
Dependability? Responsibility? Honesty? Yes, most of the copy-
book virtues of the meritocratic. But that wouldn't account
for the sense of complicity. On the evening air something else
is wafted to him, something playful, affectionate, *simpatico*,
something not too easily shocked, not too strenuously virtuous,
the smile of those who do the world's work but who don't
take the world at its own valuation — flickering, fluttering there,
complicities that enmesh him like fireflies on a summer evening.

XL

SACRIFICE TO THE MINOTAUR

Then he sailed off to the city of numbers, not the numbers
of poetry, but the numbers of car-loadings, of the through-put
of crude oil and natural gas, of the carry-over from one
crop-year to another, of the man-hours spent in punching in
rivets, or driving a bull-dozer, or conducting an orchestra —
all held together by the heroic assumption that the numbers
in the mazy labyrinth could all be squared into intricate
matrices, from which you could read off the input and output,
beneath the triumphant sign of the dollar, and, supposedly,
all tied back by an invisible thread to the spirits
exhaled by the motions of the blood, and of lymph, and of sperm.
But to him it sometimes seemed more like a Minotaur's midden.
It smelled of sulphur, of chlorine, of something inhuman.
He cried out to be delivered from the body of this death.

XLI

AMONG THE ECONOMISTS

There were some, but only a few, who could give it coherence,
with a bold flourish of free-hand extrapolation describe
a plausible future, or with brilliant equations reduce
the chaos to order, or even with a daring hypothesis
bring decades of growth and prosperity. For them, the few adepts,
the numbers formed columns in the peristyle to a temple
that rose high in the morning light, the colour of honey,
and at evening was flushed with delicate flesh-tones.
But he could only stumble in darkness, holding out his hands
to the walls to keep them from falling, feeling his way,
clasping the thread desperately, hoping it would lead him back
to the upper air and the numberless delight of human limbs,
back to all mankind's watery perfections and imperfections,
back to the unquenchable, innumerable laughter of the sea.

XLII

THESEUS NEAR DEATH

Ah, Theseus, Theseus! In the labyrinth of numbers
he would have been, if he could, a hero like Gide's Thésée,
a veteran prepared to outwit the two-headed axe
and slay the Minotaur and sail back home, having seen
everything, done everything, experienced everything, with all
his experience turned into largeness of mind, and ready
at last to rule magnanimously over a large and various
city. But the welter of numbers put the axe to that.
Suddenly there was a roar and a bellow, and the walls caved in
and a hot breath closed round his ribs, and he was gored, gored
he didn't know where but he thought in the balls, and he knew
he was close to death as he was rolled away on a stretcher.
The invisible thread was now noosed round his heart. He felt sore
and bitter. And the soreness has lasted from that day to this.

XLIII

FUTUROLOGY

The future? Leave that to those who have to design
generating-plants or weapon-systems — so would run
his sardonic advice to the rest of us after spending years
of his life trying to compose long-range economic forecasts,
most of them doomed to prove false, of course. As usual,
Pasternak got it just about right when he wrote, "We need
eternity to stand among us like a Christmas tree."
And his eternity has the bloom of the timeless present, the time
of poets and lovers, the time that takes the measure of all
searches and researches into the past and of all peering into
the future, a time whose scenarios are not of glut or shortage,
or of any of the war-games of futurology, but rather
of the apocalypse of lovers naked in each other's arms;
of trees budding, flowering, leafing; of a bird on the bough.

XLIV

SUR LE RETOUR

Even the tales of the mythical heroes tend to trail off
after the fourth or fifth adventure. But there men never seem
to grow old but go on from strength to strength until
at last they are burnt up or translated into the heavens.
They never know, a Heracles or a Theseus, the slow leaking
away of strength and daring, the gradual irrevocable
unravelling of animal pride and the tissues that nourish it,
awakening every day to new aches and twinges, that more
and more are fashioned into as intricate a system as
any other, the cardio-vascular, the gastro-intestinal, or
even the nervous system (that downward-branching tree
as you can see it in the plates to Vesalius' masterpiece).
But why go on? For in those aches, pains, twinges,
our hero knows a bell is tolling, a drum is beating.

XLV

THE BLACK PANTHER

He wakens to a tightness in his chest —
bronchitis? emphysema? lung-cancer? —
he doesn't know, but as he pads about
the flat to shave and make himself some breakfast
he feels a strange familiar in the darkness
there, a shadow mordant and malignant,
a something fanged and clawed that bides its time
and meanwhile pads about like a caged animal —
like something seen years ago in Singapore
on exhibition to the riff-raff at a pleasure-ground,
eyes blazing, muscles tensed, coiled, cramped,
the wooden bars could hardly hold it — that caged
marauder now turning into haunting image,
death the black panther now rustling in his rib-cage.

XLVI

HIS DREAMS NOW, AS SWEEPINGS

In his dreams there was once a lustre that led him on.
But now, he can't fail to notice, no green tree flourishes
in the upper air, unfading; no lizards, fanged,
are coupling in sunlight; no naked body dispenses
stark beauty and incorruption like the dead Patroclus.
The vaults with tesserae of peacock blues and greens
have faded to the grey walls of half-ruined *carceri*
where gusts of worry sweep over the traveller flying
to some distant conference – but who has forgotten where,
and has lost his brief-case, or his tickets, or his money:
dreams that are poor stuff, sweepings of a life discarded.
Where is the lady of salvation? he sighs on waking.
Where is even a glimmer of the paraclete who rescued him
when his marriage foundered, leaving him almost castaway?

XLVII

INSOMNIA

Such light as there is now comes in the watches of the night.
Contours of his life emerging through the mist like the field
of Austerlitz, when the effect of one sleeping-pill has
worn off and he's afraid to take another. Or gross sexual
fantasies uncoiling from the reptilian base of his brain
(with some cortical elaborations) and binding him fast
in lush serpentining knots of anguish and frustration
till he's forced to learn all over again how fallible
and finite (magnificent, too!) is the human intellect
and its proud works, forced to cry out from that sensual swamp
for the slow sweet rhythms of the blood and breath, forced
to cry out to be released, Oh, Christ! (And then amazed to hear
that less than a swear-word turn into a cry to the face
of the last of the gods to walk the earth, "Oh, Christ!")

XLVIII

WILD CYCLAMEN

The intolerable struggle against the bitterness of old age
and its malice, envy, jealousy. He hadn't guessed how hard
it would be to keep some tempered sweetness as physical
strength unravels; and doubly hard in a heart still riddled
with contradictions; and hardest of all, almost impossible, in
a world where there's so much shit, not only violence,
cruelty, oppression, but greed, ingratitude, hypocrisy.
Yet there are still sweet burgeonings, as rare as love or loyalty.
He's thinking of Ortona. Of the mud. Of all the poor sods
buried there, Tedeschi, Canadesi. (He's searching for something.)
Of the door of the command-post. (Yes!) Of wild cyclamen
blossoming there that spring, the buds springing serpent-
like from the earth and breaking open in delicate annunciations.
Their flowers float like tiny sails over deep-sea-green leaves.

XLIX

BIRDS OF PASSAGE

"... *et j'ai lu tous les livres.*" And so has he.
Now with his lover dead, and death slowly trickling
through all his veins and arteries, he doesn't want to read
another goddam book, they stand inert on his shelves.
Rather for him the sweet rarity in spring in Toronto
of a whitethroat singing on its way north to Georgian Bay
in that strong metre all its own, so clear, so pure,
so simple, singing to the ache in an old man's heart
of summer, and swimming-parties, and diving from the dock;
or in fall watching two hermit thrushes on their way south
hopping about and then flying up into the oak-trees,
pleased with their soft brown backs and their speckled dove-
grey breasts and their tails coloured with a dash of cinnamon,
so pleased with that pinch of cinnamon he can almost taste it.

L

VIEW TO THE WEST

So, here he roosts between the lakefront and the stockyards,
querulous, morose, sometimes a little sorry for himself,
waiting for the phone to ring, waiting, remembering,
trying to be ready for death yet to keep it at bay,
watching the gulls soar over the oak-trees and the jets
soar down to the airport, then making a little supper for
himself, perhaps reading in the paper who's in, who's out,
but not caring much any more (some Mozart is playing
over his shoulder), thinking of his two fine sons,
strong, tender, affectionate, but living so far away,
both of them inexpressibly dear to him (even sometimes
for their sake feeling a fleeting tenderness for their mother),
wondering, if he could pray, what he should pray for,
wondering if he should have another drink. But weathering it.

THE WOUNDED PRINCE

TWELVE OF THE CLOCK

Why, in the moment when the bells deliberate,
The harried heart will sometimes slacken, clench and unclench,
As slow as turbines of a ship in fog, in ice,
   Turning only for headway,

Is something never to be known by the heart
Itself, the fisted engine. But it is so. Winds
Into the labyrinthine city of the sea
   The pulsing thunder

And thins to whispers. The siren, husky, leather-lunged,
Is like a lost child crying to deaf ears of icebergs,
The wireless puts out crackling fingers and finds no friendship,
   The night comes down.

And no one can detect the beat beneath the ribs.
No vessel would be more alone in mid-Atlantic,
No horn more mournful than life-blood tapping out its message
   Through sea-dark streets.

Only the ravenous, white-lipped waves for company,
That lick the inviolate hull and ebb unfed. Only
The frosty welter and waves' black discouragement,
   Wolves of disaster.

Twelve of the clock. Now the deepest clefts, the coldest.
Where shall the eyes turn in interminable intervals
Between one bitter stroke of midnight and another
   When time seems halted;

When doors are locked and the happily married turn to each other;
When the inhuman dynamos, threading the city,
Alone keep hope alive for daybreak; when life is frozen
   And falls in pieces?

He who, awakening now or walking by the river,
Has caught the sea-smell laden with mortality
Will find no comfort left indoors. Far must he wander
  And be destitute.

He will be by the lookout's side, standing suspended
High on the moving cliff that crumbles over danger;
Beneath, the fascination of the inscrutable
  Glass of the sea;

Behind, the slippery deck; and all to lead him back
To the warmth of men and coffee steaming in the galley
A life-line, slender and often overwhelmed, braided
  Of dreams of home.

And myriad others cast eccentric from the wheel,
Outlawed by pain or grief or crime or fear of death,
Feel through the rigging the keen wind cutting, that slits the flesh
  Like surgeon's steel.

The spring comes north, the woods are blossoming with birds.
But still the invalid complains about the cold.
And it is cold. The chill is in his limbs, travelling
  Up like hemlock.

And cold the bridge where wretches stand and hesitate,
Marvelling how, when reflected, the calm of mighty stars
Seems close and easy. Constant shine below the stream
  Those tempting baubles.

Temptation has appeared in guise chameleon
To those who could not stand to be alone. The walls,
The world he has to bear like Atlas, crash down about
  The prisoner;

And some among the weeping, opiate clouds have wept;
And some, fearing the whirling blades of daylight, have hid

66

And looked for sanctuary among black-curtained cells
    Of curious lust.

All these are listed with the missing. They stare from posters
In the square; their face is known in every town
And yet not known; they wear blank anonymity
    As do the poor.

Yes, most of the poor. They are the guests unbidden,
Brought from the salt-shrewd byways to the empty hall,
Pale mouths, whose amorous, bluish lips suck up the night,
    Deep-drowned or drifting.

No wine or festal candelabra cheer the house.
There is no fireplace but the warmth of human hands.
No place of revel is this draughty casual-ward,
    Built up by bells.

But here alone can hungry creatures house at midnight.
And here must come the oceaned heart, once slackening,
To feel the bitter breath and pity, until the wheeling
    Bells are done.

O wanderer from an antique shore
Delighting in the glory of the morning,
With hair flowing and a crimson saddle-bow
And reins held lightly in a supple hand,
Stay in this defeated land,
Stay ever so,
Stay as a wonder and a warning,
Let your great chestnut rear and prance,
Rebuke the dancers in the arrested dance.

Here by the ocean evermore
Challenge the waves. Whether by luck you roamed
From fountained Delphi or the lacquered East,
As random in the woods a prince might ride
Who sought adventure far and wide
Or some rich feast;
Here where the pale green waves are combed
Gallop past tresses of starry rain,
Gallop and dazzle the waves with sun-bright mane.

And blazon the forgotten lore,
Bravado echoing to the strident clouds.
Though you have lost the country poets sung,
Stay here. Where could you ever be a stranger,
Bearing your own delight and danger
And always young?
How could you ever melt in crowds,
Roistering, laughing, scandalous, free,
Drinking the sun's strong immortality?

Here is no peace. Though swallows thread the towers
That soar themselves like swallows, like the lark,
And in the sunlight swims the holy ark
Billowed on fields of hops and garden flowers,
That droop and wait for evening. Though there is cool
Within the welling crypt; the chant comes down
In runnels, sliding on the well-worn stone
To fall in water-drops upon the pool.

Yet brings no peace. Martyrdom staining the steps,
Pain prisoned in the pillars; no chant can hide.
And underneath a greater act that seeps
Below the masonry, of One who died
In throb and sweat, Whose bloody kindness flows
Through arch and apse and buttress of this Rose.

Great bronze bells struck by the sun
  Are autumn trees,
Static — a dying civilization
  Or a frieze —
Unflawed by clamouring thoughts
  Of what's to come,
That tell their wealth, luxuriant,
  Chrysanthemum.

They sound the hour of memory
  But calmly, slowly.
The past on this late afternoon
  Converging wholly,
Folds summer weeks like starlings flying
  To thick brown leaves,
To bell-towers where a sundown city
  Last light receives.

PORTRAIT OF A YOUNG MAN

Cast back across the shoulders, the eyes see nothing.
Lovely the country of peacocks with which they dally,
Lovely but unapproachable. Sorrow
Has placed it in a tenderness of tears
Almost, or time long past. The eyes are puzzled.

Yet here is no type of weakness. Proud nerves, laced tight,
Stiffen the blood like a uniform. The eye,
The incurable connoisseur, may stray; these stand.
He, like Ulysses, his own thongs commanded.
Now see his leaning soul plucked pitiless back!

THE WOUNDED PRINCE

In the eye is the wound.

Lancings of pity, blades of sensual disappointment
Have pierced the delicate pupil.
Transfixed, the bird of heavenly airs
Is struck at sundown,
Entering the leafy wood, under the heavy lintel.

Gathered in that point all sharp humiliations;
The strokes converge.
The feathered dreams fly home from fruitless voyages.
Light needles.
Still to and fro they hawk their costliest plumage.

In your dear eye. . . .

The dark scar sings from the wanton thicket
Its princely grief;
Sets up in perilous leaves the crest of bravery;
Impaled, sings on;
Will not disown its fettering crest and crown;

So that what never could be dreamt of has been made.
From target's puny eye
Such liquid compass of this wide, aerial gaze;
From wounds, from wounds
By love inflicted, this strict and healing blade.

Thinking of you, I think of the *coureurs de bois*,
Swarthy men grown almost to savage size
Who put their brown wrists through the arras of the woods
And were lost – sometimes for months. Word would come back:
One had been seen at Crêve-coeur, deserted and starving,
One at Sault Sainte Marie shouldering the rapids.
Giant-like, their labours stalked in the streets of Quebec
Though they themselves had dwindled in distance: names only;
Rumours; quicksilvery spies into nature's secrets;
Rivers that seldom ran in the sun. Their resource
Would sparkle and then flow back under clouds of hemlock.

So you should have travelled with them. Or with La Salle.
He could feed his heart with the heart of a continent,
Insatiate, how noble a wounded animal,
Who sought for his wounds the balsam of adventure,
The sap from some deep, secret tree. But now
That the forests are cut down, the rivers charted,
Where can you turn, where can you travel? Unless
Through the desperate wilderness behind your eyes,
So full of falls and glooms and desolations,
Disasters I have glimpsed but few would dream of,
You seek new Easts. The coats of difficult honour,
Bright with brocaded birds and curious flowers,
Stowed so long with vile packs of pemmican,
Futile, weighing you down on slippery portages,
Would flutter at last in the courts of a clement country,

Where the air is silken, the manners easy,
Under a guiltless and reconciling sun.

You hesitate. The trees are entangled with menace.
The voyage is perilous into the dark interior.
But then your hands go to the thwarts. You smile. And so
I watch you vanish in a wood of heroes,
Wild Hamlet with the features of Horatio.

No monuments or landmarks guide the stranger
Going among this savage people, masks
Taciturn or babbling out an alien jargon
And moody as barbaric skies are moody.

Berries must be his food. Hurriedly
He shakes the bushes, plucks pickerel from the river,
Forgetting every grace and ceremony,
Feeds like an Indian, and is on his way.

And yet, for all his haste, time is worth nothing.
The abbey clock, the dial in the garden,
Fade like saint's days and festivals.
Months, years, are here unbroken virgin forests.

There is no law — even no atmosphere
To smooth the anger of the flagrant sun.
November skies sting, sting like icicles.
The land is open to all violent weathers.

Passion is not more quick. Lightnings in August
Stagger, rocks split, tongues in the forest hiss,
As fire drinks up the lovely sea-dream coolness.
This is the land the passionate man must travel.

Sometimes — perhaps at the tentative fall of twilight —
A belief will settle that waiting around the bend
Are sanctities of childhood, that melting birds
Will sing him into a limpid gracious Presence.

The hills will fall in folds, the wilderness
Will be a garment innocent and lustrous

To wear upon a birthday, under a light
That curls and smiles, a golden-haired Archangel.

And now the channel opens. But nothing alters.
Mile after mile of tangled struggling roots,
Wild-rice, stumps, weeds, that clutch at the canoe,
Wild birds hysterical in tangled trees.

And not a sign, no emblem in the sky
Or boughs to friend him as he goes; for who
Will stop where, clumsily constructed, daubed
With war-paint, teeters some lust-red manitou?

CANOE-TRIP

What of this fabulous country
Now that we have it reduced to a few hot hours
And sun-burn on our backs?
On this south side the countless archipelagoes,
The slipway where titans sent splashing the last great glaciers;
And then up to the foot of the blue pole star
A wilderness,
The pinelands whose limits seem distant as Thule,
The millions of lakes once cached and forgotten,
The clearings enamelled with blueberries, rank silence about
      them;
And skies that roll all day with cloud-chimeras
To baffle the eye with portents and unwritten myths,
The flames of sunset, the lions of gold and gules.
Into this reservoir we dipped and pulled out lakes and rivers,
We strung them together and made our circuit.
Now what shall be our word as we return,
What word of this curious country?

It is good,
It is a good stock to own though it seldom pays dividends.
There are holes here and there for a gold-mine or a hydro-plant.
But the tartan of river and rock spreads undisturbed,
The plaid of a land with little desire to buy or sell.
The dawning light skirls out its independence;
At noon the brazen trumpets slash the air;
Night falls, the gulls scream sharp defiance;
Let whoever comes to tame this land, beware!
Can you put a bit to the lunging wind?
Can you hold wild horses by the hair?
Then have no hope to harness the energy here,
It gallops along the wind away.
But here are crooked nerves made straight,

The fracture cured no doctor could correct.
The hand and mind, reknit, stand whole for work;
The fable proves no cul-de-sac.
Now from the maze we circle back;
The map suggested a wealth of cloudy escapes;
That was a dream, we have converted the dream to act.
And what we now expect is not simplicity,
No steady breeze, or any surprise,
Orchids along the portage, white water, crimson leaves.
Content, we face again the complex task.

And yet the marvels we have seen remain.
We think of the eagles, of the fawns at the river bend,
The storms, the sudden sun, the clouds sheered downwards.
O so to move! With such immaculate decision!
O proudly as waterfalls curling like cumulus!

There is water at my feet
Moving through the shadowed bridge.
It coils and melts in silence, glides
A monarch from the realm of darkness.

Where have I seen that same dark beauty,
The smooth glister along its back
So self-possessed and final? Where
Have I seen it trail its invitation?

It spreads slowly and broadens past
The arches, ample for any burden
To take and mingle with itself,
Yet goes straight on, makes no entreaty.

For what has it to do with me
Or with this city?   It comes from caves
That we know nothing of, twisting
In reluctance from the earth,

And flows unmoved by midnight bells,
Listening to no sound except
Its own, seeing no other face,
While absent from its own dominion.

Spear this wind within your mind.
It will pass with eagle swiftness
While the bloom of heaven's vineyard
Fades and leaves no wine behind.

Snare the bird with cunning art.
It has come from some white fastness
Where it soared and rested freely.
It will perish in your heart.

Grieve not when it flutters dead.
Though you see them not for rain-clouds
There are more above the streaming.
Take and eat your daily bread.

METEORS

Down, down they come on earth's cold shores
Like mallards winged by gun-shot.
And though the leisurely moon-moistened flesh
Protests, the keener intellect
Slinks not to heel.

For stars have stung remembrance falling,
Dropping like tired flocks of birds,
Breaking the curtain momentarily
Before the icy plummet to destruction.
And seemed to say,
"Search, speculate —
Whence came the frost along our wings?"

So that the mind alerted, seeks,
Searchlights the sky,
Is sure there must be somewhere
Wings or a wrack of feathers
To recover.
Or, at the least, grey monstrous waves
Of some forbidden sea.

But while the heart works frozen,
Sends down the great aorta snow,
Truth dawns. There is no wrack, no sea,
Nothing whose duplicate lies in the memory,
Nothing.

And yet if thought retires exhausted,
Droops, waits for its morning ration,
It is not duped.
It recognized the foe it never knew,
It snuffed the savour of annihilation.

Not this oblivion you gave before.
Green water sliding down like light on leaves,
Hushed edge of crystal, glass that never grieves
The eye by mirroring, were then a door
   That opened into singing groves.

It must be something different now, not joy's
Forgetfulness. Your only anodyne
Entombment, hiss on hills of granite rain;
Drowned clappers calling, melting, of bell-buoys
   Murmuring, lost too far down for pain.

Say no word.
There is no wisdom can be said
With wisdom's sapphire palely spread
Foldless and faultless overhead
And on the water.

Hush! no song.
The sweetest song would be profane.
The moon's own melody like rain
Descends; set out a cup for rain,
Your hollowed heart.

And then be still.
Remembering our mean estate,
Let us be last to celebrate
But wait as chastened children wait
The word of pardon.

SONNET

How shall I find love's octave, the modest string
That answers to the wishes of the dumb?
I had believed speech easily would come,
Issuing as water; so I could sing
The liquid gamut of imagining.
But I am new arrived in this sweet kingdom,
The old use clings, the mind is troublesome,
My satisfaction seems a buried thing.

There is the song of white-throats through the land;
I sing within. The overarching bright
Blue sky, horizoned as the robin's egg,
Describes my hope. To make you understand,
Those tones of borrowed eloquence I beg,
Wood full of birds, bending of morning light.

DIAMOND

I saw your eyes tonight, deep blue;
Sad truly, but so only made
More clear like water in the shade
Where boys peer down for bass or trout.
And so I peered to fathom you.

My gaze was far from touching ground.
Fast sloped the opal sides away
And further down assurance lay,
So that my line was all let out
With deeper caverns still to sound.

But yet joy! joy! for what I found.
Your lovely silence uttered more
Than stubborn lips would say before
And, flowering everywhere about,
Lay prisoned pearl and diamond.

There in the quiet water, shown
By sorrow vulnerable and dear,
Shone forth immaculate the fear
No glance can ever violate,
Your secret self like watered stone.

No music is abroad except your breath,
That comes and goes and gives the night its dream.
The hawks have done their sun-down flights, the wind
Drops down now Scorpio's coils are on the trees;
Cones dropping and the far-off whip-poor-wills
Are bubbles in a deep and noiseless stream.

The blush of moonlight lasts and lightens,
The queen of heaven makes the water blue
As birds; the sky bends down, the islands gather,
The hour's repose is deep as yours. I turn
To where your head is lying, dreaming of skies
As calm as these; and see you motionless
In moonlight, a quiet isle in quiet seas.

OUTCAST ISLANDS

There are islands where no birds will build
Except the tern.
And it flies clamouring all day long
Its cry the restlessness of hunger.
Disappointed as it drops for fish
A hundred times it mounts and tries again,
And so from morn till dark
Scorning the gull's parabola,
It whirs, whips, strikes, and cuts the air,
And when night falls lies down on rock.

To some the islands are mirage,
They ride so far from shore
And there is little at the best to see –
Sand, a few abortive bushes –
Grim underneath the gnarled storms
And when the sun shines, sterile.

But there they stand firm, fixed,
And no mirage,
Though some are lucky not to know them.
For them there can be no event,
No novelty to break the emptiness
That holds as at the world's first morning.
Their own wild terns, the gulls, the sea,
Make all the music that is made
Or sometimes ducks returning from the feeding-grounds
At dawning.

Though far, far, from your green valley,
Remember them sometimes.
Rocks and ledges have been creature's homes,

Turn to them with your easy charity.
And yet
(Since I am jealous of any shadow on your pillow,
And this might tarnish golden hair)
Let them not linger
In the mind's twilit thoroughfare;
Let them pass lightly
Like childhood bogies long outgrown,
Pass, and be only half-believed in
Like sailors' tales of whitening bones.

A VISION

Uprooted did the tree appear,
Yet flourished glistering and bold.
It fed upon the atmosphere,
Breathing and exhaling gold.

And twigs fell weighted from the boughs,
That lately had been flushed with bud.
They left a wound for light to close
And, as they fell, they turned to blood.

Was this a sign of havoc coming,
This hieratic show I dreamed,
This primitive and perfect mumming?
Like ichor through the air it streamed.

And were the leaves the tears of gods
For boys to whom the guns are calling
With only youth and grace for odds
And hair the sunlight is enthralling?

If such it was, then show of lies
Like every pity for man's pain
That folds about the anguished eyes
The treacherous cloths of sunshot rain.

No lustre will involve the sky
When nerve-stitched flesh is blown to bits.
Uncomforted, like animals, cry
Women whom destruction visits.

Imagination grew the tree
To mock the way weak men have bled.
Evasion turned to heraldry
The living, sweet, imperfect red.

THE GODDESS

Imagine a portrait painted in tempera:
The full, round limbs against a background the colour of corn;
Blue sky drawn smooth in perfect urbanity;
The sun, controlling all the distance,
Rolled also about the feet of the speechless goddess;
And on the figure the nimbus of contentment,
Arms, breasts, and lips draped in a full-bosomed smile.

This would be Peace,
This would recall the sprawling villages
Where after a bountiful harvest the shocks of corn
Hang yellowing on the southern wall;
Where all day grunt and sweat the labouring oxen,
But, once come nightfall,
Crickets sing in the busiest cart-track,
The church-clock strikes,
And soon there is nowhere a light to be seen.

These were the dwellings in which you delighted,
The seats appointed for your homely but elegant progress.
You would go barefoot round from one to one,
Granting to all your benediction,
Till the grapes grew sweet beneath the sheltering leaves,
The women ripened like a fruitful vine.
But the villages have retreated, have taken to the hills.
And now we wonder if you have gone with them; are you hidden
As men hide the crown-jewels through a long campaign?
Or, instructed by the regularity
In our own still veins, shall we look elsewhere?
To search through the highland settlements might profit little,
We left them so long ago, they are now so alien.
And there is still another place to try, there remains
The centre of energy.
After preliminary clatter and fumbling,

The yards passed, the switches pawed lightly aside,
The driving-wheels assert their steady purpose.
After superficial flutterings
The blades evaporate into thin air.

Only the whirling, steady shaft is left like stone.

When the skies close,
When light has the eerie colour of a bruise,
When the heavy light tastes leaden on the tongue;
And the brave, deserted by all heavenly healers,
Are dying slowly into desperation;
When the shrunk light stiffens, mortifies –
Eclipse, crows call, quacks swarm along the streets –
In the yawning hour of funeral,
In plague

Still to remember the patience of the fiery artificers,
Who morning after morning from their own lips blew the reluctant
          flames;
Who, asking nothing of the bright seraphim,
Through the murkiest days shaped their gold images,
Fashioned them trophies, tripods, cups, libation bowls,
And trusted they would reappear; who failed often
But, always imagining some perfect icon, calm, reserved,
To resurrect the light, achieved it sometimes;
Who, believing in luck, were not embittered.
They looked up. But the nihilist heavens did not appal them.
They went about their work, making the metal ductile,
Hammering it into curious shapes, annealing, burnishing,
Intent about the smithy, blowing it to the pitch
Of their quick zeal. Their breath was ardent, flickering,
A Pentecost that played about the senseless mass
And conquered it. But like a lover. And would not rest.

Until one lucky morning, casually looking up.
No longer the hiatus;
The heavenly company!
Wing-tip to wing-tip, again in kind surveillance
To come at the call of the beaten, the oppressed,

92

Healers, to breathe into the sick an irrational hope.
The death-cloth plucked from the face of the dead day,
A miracle!
Flowers springing up in place of spotted leprosy,
Warmth glancing, pouring on the ulcered earth,
Joy coming out in every leaf and bough.
And there
Where mists unravelling reveal the mountain,
The sacred mountain where the vision flows,
The source, the head, the dayspring manifest,
Intelligence-and-Power, the lost archangel.

We who watched you walking on the water
Now tenderly salute your desperate parting.
If anywhere you hear our sheltered tears,
Be comforted. We do not blame. Strong men,
Who trusted in the earth, have ghastly fallen;
Priests, before the people celebrating,
Ghostly within the shrine have paled and fled.
You were alone. You were not strong.

You had the tissues of a girl, yet could
Not be content with home and husbandry.
Dangerous as water was the path you chose.
You felt the city at your finger-tips,
Took its full charge, its jagged crises, played
With its brittle lightnings, sent out continually
The rhythm of your heart to master them,
Kept among static, sirens, air compressors,
Kept in the city the beautiful slowness of breathing.

We wondered. Baffled by lights, humiliated
By mad machines, by schedules, we asked
What were the angels that breathed into you their peace,
That, hovering above you, gave you strength. We gazed
And prayed and agonized, afraid lest you
Would lose your footing on those slippery seas.
But, as day followed day, we grew more confident.
We believed. You would not fail. You would arrive
At some new Fortunate Islands and bring us to you.

And then the spasm. A catch in the side, the throat
Constricted, breathlessness as the genius left you,
Blood pouring in a haemorrhage, the feet unsteady,
Down, down you slipped, your virtue lost like bubbles.
Now through the gates of mirror and mirage

We look and grieve. For you there were no islands,
No skies enscrolled with veined and vivid green.
Pain was your vocation and achievement,
The restless sea your anthemed citadel.
But where the waters have gone over you,
Flashing shines still your dying, ransomed gift,
The blue aurora weapon of the future,
Jewelled hope and dangerous dawn, Excalibur.
The temper of the sensitive and strong.

Always the path leads back.
The spy who has spun his web as subtly as an artist,
Living in a perpetual cellar, a prey to whispers,
Finds at last that the schemes he has excreted, the work of the
    spider,
Are fastened at some point to the visible world; and endangered
    and violable.
Or the criminal, working at night,
Who slunk as a boy into crime like an endless subway,
Somewhere is careless and, caught by his finger-tips,
Must leave the grey light of no-man's land and stagger back,
Back through humanity's brutal barriers.
Always the path leads back.

Or the counterfeiter, following his species of madness.
His eyes, enflamed by the colour of coins,
His imagination, corroded by golden calculations,
Tell him his room, transmuted by spurious flames to gold,
Is an image of the whole dark golden globe
Where his fears are irrelevant. Yet there in the darkness,
Surrounded by greed as by a neurosis, he still is afraid.
For always, though sooner or later, will come the knock on the
    door;
Always the path leads back.

In hospitals too there are those who live underground,
Who thrill to the delightful chills of fever,
Sweating in the sweet drift of chloroform or ether.
And there they have time for their hobbies. Turning the
    hospital into a hot-house,
Where their dreams can sprout to enormous blooms,
Lilies, overpowering lilacs, fleshly dahlias,

They feed their flowers with the flesh of their friends.
But sometimes the longest convalescence must come to an end.

Even the lovers living on their island
Must kiss the friendly earth good-bye like children.
All summer long they swooned an ecstasy away,
Bound in a mesh the warblers wove with their bright bits of song.
But now the leaves are falling, the distant surf is calling,
The summer sun is over.
Always the path leads back;
The islands are a prelude to the shore,
The dawn wind stirs the curtains and blows in the light,
The subway opens on the public square.

On dust. On sparrows bathing in the dust. On dust, heat, noise.
There in the market-place where tongues clack and chaffer
Under the actual sun, to the sound of clocks,
Are brass bursts of light, and draymen cursing,
Sharps of sirens, and brakes and gears, and pistons drumming.
Are shouts — and not the long voluptuous silence
Or bird-calls issuing from the arras of a dream.
But there steel-bright necessity. Out of those notes,
That sound so improbable, to weld a music like
        a school-boy's song,
Out of those metals to hammer, to conquer, the new and
        strenuous song.

IMAGE OF SILENUS

"He is like one of the images of Silenus.
They are made to open in the middle, and
inside them are figures of the gods."

(Plato, *Symposium*

Suddenly lifting and rising heavily from the reeds,
Its bent legs trailing and bent neck outstretched,
With wide wings set like sails,
Comes the great blue heron.
It is as if, in the twilight, a whole ship should be startled from the
     stream
And, limping a little at first, then gaining assurance,
Should continue across the sky imperturbably;
Equally at home in the brown shadows of evening and the moss-
     soft shadowy trees
As among the fish-haunted weeds and the lily-pads.
It leaves no wake, it makes no noise,
It flaps in time with the slow fall of night.
And yet unmistakably a wonder,
Unmistakably blue among the indistinguishable limbs and
     boughs.

So that the weather-beaten mask, that sees everything,
That has the air of having seen it all before,
Is taken by surprise.
The strained grin has been rivered by marks of rain
Since first it was set up in the garden; it is not so bright now
As when it left the hands of the makers; one would not know
It had any treasures to show, it opens so seldom.
But its population is many and waiting.
They are lodged underground among tombs,

Baffled, bewildered, at a turn of the catacombs.
Now, as the mask relaxes and the door unaccountably opens,
They appear.

See them, the shrunken figures of desire,
Swarming complete as when they were first here deposited,
But not heroic, filling all the sky,
Miniatures rather, toys in a toy shop window.
See Dionysus and the golden Christopher,
Francis circled by a charm of birds,
Apollo of the large loose limbs and gauze-gold nimbus,
Foam-born Aphrodite.
And all the other roles that men have pictured for themselves,
The figures fashioned out of desperation,
The plants they grew to feed their failure,
All throng behind the ironic mask.
The runner here is always first to breast the tape,
The infant Hercules compels the snake,
The surgeon cuts the flesh to an exquisite thinness,
The climber stands triumphant over Everest.

And other figures, neither gold nor simple,
Tell of the ultimate wish to do and suffer.
Green light escaping from clouds portending thunder
Shines on the prince at Elsinore, shines on the dungeoned
        Oedipus.

(Stand off a little, or you will see those blasted eyes.)

And even far off there will come,
Faintly perhaps, dissonant, confused,
But gradually forming into words,
Complaint of captives,
Lament of long-denied desires,
Strange heave and swell, unmusical, of all this ill-assorted choir.

        O where is the realm of promised good,
        The hint of content we have felt in the blood?

We have been told of the bird on the bough,
Of the misted land where time goes slow.
Sometimes we thought that high in the air
We saw it drift. But where? O where?

The mask has said, "Your hopes defer;
As seeds are still, so do not stir."
But sweet in the dark is the sickly doubt,
What if we never should blossom out?
What if the promise were puffs of air?
Where is our city? Nowhere? Nowhere?

And the bird? Is it only a blue mirage,
To waken desire and helpless rage?
There is no secret to which it flies.
There is no bird; the wonder dies.
Let us go down the deathward stair,
Give us your hand, despair, despair.

The song scatters.
The words are dissolved like a cloud into snowflakes.

And then out of the silence comes answering, not a song —
It has no words, it is animal, inarticulate —
A ground swell continually making for the shores of speech
And never arriving. And like the sea variable,
Unpredictable, not fixed in one place,
But gathering everywhere a vagrant strength.
From whispers in narrow alleys,
From sighs confided to lonely pillows,
From mutterings and grumblings as the bars are closing.
Yes, this is the real and suffering city.
Turn and look down from the railway viaduct.
They are souls underground, buried under miles of brick,
Under miles of chimneys. They are rows of jostling seeds,
Planted too close, unlikely to come to maturity.
Some will shoot up (germs are brave things and hard to kill)
But most will be crushed; and, living, will not even know

100

Why they had no chance to break and expand;
Will not even be able to put their discontent into words.
Only sometimes at nightfall, like this, they will sigh and know
       they are beaten.

Their sigh comes and goes with the night-wind.
The wind drops.
And now the whole city is quiet,
Under the halo of man-made twilight.

And to the inner city, the city of phantoms,
The winds of chance at last are charitable.
Open it has been, but guarded by guiling glass
By an invisible barrier. The puppets have looked out
Like sick children with their faces pressed to the window.
Now the blinds drop, the shop shuts, the mask grins again.

For the great bird
With wings stretched wide as love
Has disappeared.
It is travelling on slow through the clinging darkness,
Or somewhere has found its home
And moored
In its nest that quietly floats on the sea-dark forest,
Now everywhere perfectly sealed and secret.

THE NET AND THE SWORD

TUSCAN VILLA

As the winds veer
The weathervane smiles
But the bell in the lofty belfry
No longer tells the hour
In the sunlight perfect as a tear.
And, if it did,
Would the soldiers crunching the tiles,
Would the soldiers listen
Or the doves that under the broad eaves harbour?

Unblinking sphinx with the sunlight goring its flanks
The villa stares over the undulant plain
Past the new-made graves and the tanks upturned like beetles
Past the poplars dozing in the river-valley
And the flickering, fiery tongues of the olive trees
Hazily, to where a cypressed campanile
Or rosy duomo has become irrelevant fuzz
In a pair of binoculars, too dim to provide the guns
With a reference-object or add to a new triangulation.
But there at the periphery persists some old
Enigma, exhaled long ago like a smile or a gesture,
That the villa dallies with, dallies and drops,
In dotage forgetting the key to its own conundrum.
Embrowned with the years, embrasured, bastioned,
It has lost the key down a well or left it in
A bricked-up casemate, and is now too old, too torpid
To care. Explosions seep through the thick walls as rumours.
What little is left of the villa's heart beats slow,
Integuments hardening inwards, all orifices
Closing. Daydreaming towards its end,
How should it hear that the plain is swelling and heaving,
That not far off shells are spouting like whales,
That the landscape is shifting; how should it know
That its own walls have become only

Scaffolding for artillery observations,
Its tower the platform for a survey of destruction?

> *The straw-thin winds*
> *That float over the tower*
> *Are grist to the grating weathervane*
> *As it cockily struts and grins.*
> *Why is it strange, it creaks, for one species of power*
> *To follow another?*
> *The end of an age,*
> *And the end of an afternoon*
> *Are one and the same to grinding fortune.*

Unfortunate order; the architecture of a flower
That drew from the rooted peasants oil and wine
To be involved in the whorled extravagance
Of gallery, chapel, chamber, tower and orchard,
Folding their deep splendours privily
To hide a few in vivid leaves of light.
Music was here; and at a time of festival
Four seasons seemed to circle round a maypole
Streamered with joys that the dancers twirled and untwirled
In the candid light exulting. But not for joys
And feast-days only accompaniment stood by.
Before the music stopped, the flower grew blowsy,
Resided in these spaces resonance
Waiting to catch and liquefy each heart-beat;
The chapel soothed and purified remorse;
Under the entrance-arch regret like a cry
Could curl, as the coachman (huzza!) drove off with a flourish;
Emblems of victorious pride and death
Went echoing through the garden – green laurel leaves
And peacocks – as aids to meditation; a belvedere
Announced the prospect of a lucid future
Where rows of cypresses as confidants
Sponged up a loiterer's melancholy; and when
In a summer night against an open casement
Rustled along the balustrade the play

Of hands and voices, the illuminated gallery
Sounding with those lost and wooded flutes
Breathed out the subtlest perfume of young love.

> *But the crunch of a hob-nailed boot*
> *Has a resonance all its own*
> *Crisping a summer day with winter*
> *Confounding the season,*
> *Whether the foot*
> *That shatters the red-clay tiles*
> *Be Punic, Lombard, Hun,*
> *The ravishing tread that hunts for loot*
> *Be Visigoth or Canadian.*

Ransacked now. The boots track upstairs and down
And in my lady's chamber. Rivered and ravaged
The stairways, drifting with table-cloths, withered letters,
Splayed, worm-spliced leaves of ancient wisdom,
A fragment of a children's hobby-horse,
All, all adrift with the flotsam of four centuries.
Was there some vileness lurking understairs,
Infection curled in the bud before it flowered,
That brought this dreadful cleansing on the house?
Say, rather, with a level voice, that the corpse
Of a dying house like the corpse of a man is vile;
And many a cause of death remains obscure.
But dying it is. Death in its brains and loins.
The fowler has loosed in the loft the doors of the cages;
The dove-cote, where crossing wings would silver and glide,
Deserted, presents only the guano stare of vacuity,
The birds have vanished like thoughts from a calcined skull.
And in the bowels of the house clot deadly humours,
The surfeit of garlanded years kept locked in the dark,
Furs, faience, crystal, silver, jewels,
A fistula soon to be broken in exquisite riot.
Death, finally. The dark cornucopia
Where the patron past dropped treasure lavishly,
Is corrupted by its own confined effulgence,

Is fouled with droppings, with the harvest of decay,
Is dank as a well full of years, as a well full of leaves.

What should the bell in the belfry say
Where the Madonna in low relief
Blest and divided the ordered day?
This is the moment of stasis,
Secular, silent with unbelief,
And timeless as a wilderness.
The cords are broken. No grief
From a passing-bell
Tells that a time-brimmed villa ebbs away.

Mildness that holds its mirror to departing breath,
Whose feathered winds attend to whisper if
The villa lives or no, this sky of limpid mildness
Has been invaded time and time again,
Has suffered Visigoths and Saracens,
Scarred by catastrophe but still serene.
Untimely peace bends over the shifting field
Embracing, as it seems, the pain that wounds it,
Charming the air. Far up reconnaissance planes
Are motionless and hang on strings, while shell-bursts
Drift down-wind and milkweed parachutes
Flower silkily. O calm entelechy
In which the soldiers on the tower are held!
Entelechy of silken peace and light!
That fastens actors on the lofty stage,
Emerged from winding ladders to this moment
By a dank trap-door. On history's monstrous back
(Their instruments set up to scan the future
And plot the guns in parallel) they ride
As harpooneers a moribund leviathan,
Dabbling their feet in the crisped light that curls
Everywhere evenly, steadily; and sail scot-free,
Sail where the sun is scotched and quickly healed.
Surely this is not out of God's grace,
Where soldiers and a dying tower are lapped in peace.

The doves that death has dispossessed
Cling to the outward wall.
They will be scattered wide and lost.
Peace will come, if it come at all,
As an exiled bird with wounded breast.
The waves so rough
On the angry fields that truce
Can only fall
Like a prismed tear on a ravaged face.

Gaze deeper, then, still deeper into this limpid sky
Till the even grain is refracted into garish fire,
Stampeding, raging from the dark corona;
Fire-falls and veils that scythe and sway; cascades
Of blazing vapour when the heavens open;
Insinuating flames between the bricks and cornice,
Picking the bones of villas, skulls and voices,
Consuming ode and palinode and elegy,
Eating the salvo-smoke of human aims.
This will appear — though not to the theodolite
The soldiers swing or to a dying house —
Perpetual fire where lives like salt are spilt,
Fire where the earth is burning like a bush,
All-trampling fire by which new towers are raised,
Designer of wide-flowering stone and secret cells,
That charges through unrusted wheat
To burst its riddle in the kernelled ear,
That swirls and boils in the cup of the unripe grape,
That castles builds in the blood like ropes of sand,
That castles burns, and boils in a peasant's loins.
Violent the sea of fire the soldiers sail,
Too tightly closed in a luxury of flame,
Too softly stroked by a lion's paw

To see the blood in the flood of brightness
Or know themselves as the scars the sky devours.

> *Winds veer*
> *And the weathervane veers*
> *And the instruments are packed away.*
> *But the crown with diaphanous veils*
> *Of fire*
> *Over the tower*
> *And the trampled field prevails*
> *And will prevail that far-off day*
> *When other towers are circled by mild birds.*

Just out of reach they glimmer like a globe,
A plaything for a boy, as round as promised pleasure,
But coloured with a different, luscious century,
Another world that riflemen make eyes at
From underneath steel helmets,
From underneath dry, spurious leaves they wear.

Trudging in single file through unsexed drought,
They whistle the fruit to modify the season,
With dusty voices supplicate green trees
To slake their thirst. But no streams break the heat,
No tantalizing, sweet
Drops stain the webbing of their discipline.

Still the thought of juice buds sweet on their tongues.
     Shoving
The lips of the beckoning fruit apart (a stinger
Like a wasp's probes deep for swooning nectar)
They sluice the sweetness out of their mouths till cool
Along their thighs they feel
A trickle of the girls they dream of loving.

At a momentary halt some break the branches,
Wolf down the fleshy liquor, which a few enjoy
But wonder what it is, a peach or orange?
And then a whistle blows. They fill their tunics
And slinging rifles, packs
And bren-guns, move forward into mortar range.

Tonight when digging parties comb the salient
Many a thin-skinned orient orb of sense,

A globe as soft as hand grenades are hard,
Will glimmer in untasted opulence
Crushed to the avid breasts
Of striplings, now wandering through a darkened orchard.

See how he adjusts his scarf as we move off
And, looking back along the waiting trucks,
Out of some distant past lifts up his glove
And smiles. The tawny sunlight falls archaic.

And stiffening with him in a ritual
Of battle we all get rolling, his scout-car leading.
As always, he is spruce and casual
And looks like someone going to a wedding.

He might be mated with the lion sun
Or with disaster, the paramour of beasts
Aprowl and coupling in this desolation
Where fallen tiles throw light on famished lusts.

The day waits. Is quiet as a ruined column.
Then, high up, air-bursts black as vultures in a moment
Suck all substance from the heavenly volume.
Listen! At last in the ditch the whine of shell-fragments.

And we sad lackeys wonder what comes next.
Is the ruin ahead or behind us? Does the road lead forward
Or back? His gaze alone is unperplexed.
He sips from this thin air some sacred word.

Through all his veins the sacrament of danger,
Discovering secret fires, runs riot. His hard
Eyes gleam with cunning pressed from smouldering hunger;
His coat burns sleek and lilied as a leopard's.

Whether some lucky chance has made him think
That glaze invulnerable or whether he puts

His pride before his life — and ours are linked —
Who knows? We only know we hate his guts.

The region is hermetic, though, and strange
And as he leads us to the holocaust
Our blood as well is volatized and changed.
Our dawning search is lit by wars long past.

Now as he crests the turret to sweep and lick
The landscape, snakes glittering back a wanton joy
Like a slick of flame from a hit petrol-truck
That in no time can ribbon through a convoy.

Crisp daggers naked in the daylight. Flash
Blue with Arcturus, crimsoned with Antares.
Diamonds, discharged from icy poles, gash
The frothed flesh with thrust of secret sympathies,

And, in our entrails twisting venomous truth,
Shriek that the star-wide world is desperate, desperate —
Fanged festival of stars from a serpent's mouth
Blazing us breathless to the Lion Gate.

AN INCIDENT

Arrange the scene with only a shade of difference
And he would be a boy in his own native
And fern-fronded providence,
With a map in his hand, searching for a portage overgrown
With brush. Slim he is as a moccasin-flower
With his throat open
To the winds, to the four winds, quivering,
Who alone by the worm-holed flower of the rose-pink house
Bears the weight of this many-ringed, foreign noon,
Shadowless, vast and pitiless.
Notched by the wedge of his frown, it takes no notice.
Light that, alive, would be pungent with resin,
Sapless, now weighs and ponders like limestone.

What is he waiting for
As he studies a map the colour of his youth?
Time stops and whirs in his ear like a hummingbird
As he gazes this way and that
For someone to relieve him
For someone to break through the thicket of his isolation.

In the silence
The grasshoppers crackle and crumble the summer
Between their thin wings
And their singing thighs.
And his head has begun to sing,
To sing with the heat.
Stampeding, his blood butts him like a bull-calf.
How should one so young have learned how to wait?

Ah! there is the relief.
A stray round has caught him at the nape of the neck

And splayed him flat on the earth,
His blood flung wide as a sunburst.

And the pink house, that eavesdropped
Through smoke-blackened holes to each palpitation,
Recovering its reserve,
Sucks in unblemished stillness;
While the wise light with petrified foliage
Having disposed of this awkward animal tremor
Again stands superb as a temple.

THE NET AND THE SWORD

Who could dispute his choice
That in the nets and toils of violence
Strangled his leafing voice
Enforced his own compassionate heart to silence,
Hunted no more to find the untangling word
And took a short, straight sword?

In this sandy arena, littered
And looped with telephone wires, tank-traps, mine-fields,
Twining about the embittered
Debris of history, the people whom he shields
Would quail before a stranger if they could see
His smooth as silk ferocity.

Where billowing skies suspend
Smoke-latticed rumours, enmeshed hypotheses,
And mad transmitters send
Impossible orders on crossed frequencies,
His eyes thrust concentrated and austere.
Behind his lids, the skies are clear.

Not that he ever hopes
To strike the vitals of the knotted cloud.
But, to the condemned, those ropes
At least let in the sun. And he, grown proud,
Among the sun's bright retinue would die,
Whose care is how they fall, not why.

In this air
Breathed once by artist and *condottier*,
Where every gesture of proud men was nourished,
Where the sun described heroic virtue and flourished
Round it trumpet-like, where the face of nature
Was chiselled by bright centuries hard as sculpture;
His face on this clear air and arrogant scene,
Decisive and impenetrable, is Florentine.

Where every hill
Is castled, he stands like a brooding tower; his will
An angry shadow on this cloudless sky,
Gold with the dust of many a panoply
And blazonings burnt up like glittering leaves;
His only cognizance his red-patched sleeves;
Fair hair his helmet; his glancing eye, the swagger
Of his stride are gallant's sword and dagger.

And in his mind
The sifting, timeless sunlight would not find
Memories of stylish Florence or sacked Rome,
Rather the boyhood that he left at home;
Skating at Scarborough, summers at the Island,
These are the dreams that float beyond his hand,
Green, but estranged across a moat of flame;
And now all bridges blown the way he came.

No past, no future
That he can imagine. The fiery fracture
Has snapped that armour off and left his bare
Inflexible, dark frown to pluck and stare
For some suspected rumour that the brightness sheds

Above the fruit-trees and the peasants' heads
In this serene, consuming lustrousness
Where trumpet-tongues have died, and all success.

Do not enquire
What he has seen engrained in stillest fire
Or what he purposes. It will be well.
We who have shared his exile can trumpet-tell
That underneath his wild and frowning style
Such eagerness has burned as could not smile
From coats of lilies or emblazoned roses.
No greater excellence the sun encloses.

LINES FOR A COMBATANT

"Destroy us if you will, so long as
it is in the light."

(Homer, *Iliad* XVII.697)

So . . . with the cry of Ajax brassed about
My tunic, having made my peace from brittleness,
To the air committed ambition, expectation,
My soul, even, that flickers above me fitfully,
I wait here in the olive-grove . . . "to die,
To die so long as it is in the light. . . . "
Flame from a guttering text in gold ascending
Is rolled with the noon-day haze from the dust of battle,
A candle in broad day with gold smoke contending
Imposes on the smoke pride's transitive vigour,
Bends round the breast a conscious cuirass
Of constantly dissolved and reconstructed rigour,
Breastwork of fire to conquer fire, brass
Cymbals beating to keep savagery at bay
Where a litter of lions ramps in the valley.

So I am free to observe from my sun-drenched ambush
How past the leafy ridge the world ends.
The valley drops in a glittering lacuna,
Meridian void that offers to nested gladiators
Nothing spectacular, dust and dry lightnings only
In an absurd, outstretched arena, a circus
Of phantoms. And surely it is absurd
To attempt to print on turbulence, that strips
The leaves from the trees and the drops of sex, what lips
May fallibly form into an incised word
Of strenuous calm. Into the hectoring chaos
Have thousands passed (and most of them safely)
Folly surely to think that, if there be loss,

The blood's percussive modes at all could qualify
This vacuous fire in a desert place.

Yet, obstinate, the heart will have it
That pride can infect the void with limits,
By inbreathing turbulence with a quiet mind
Can transmit the future vehemently;
That unless is built a brittle glittering glacis,
Drummed into the air volleys of scattering brightness,
Unless in the air the powdered breath is mustered,
No showers will fall to make the new shoots bear,
Nor the ransomed spring swell new buds with its sighing.

Weaves in the sun the ceaseless argument
And while with each breath the bright lattice weaves, unweaves,
I watch (with a slight feeling of unease,
As though the music were too strident) how
Above a grey-green well swells a ripe fig-tree,
Its leaf-planes vanes in the light breeze slightly turning
Till I wonder if it is they that please me, or the thought
Of myself years on, remembering the light through the fig-tree.

I am become brittle, brittle, a breaking sentence
On the lip of silence. I am almost self-consumed.
Pride's intellectual empire now has for defence
The linked breastwork of animal assertion;
But underneath the carapace are ventricles bone dry.
Apprehension of an improbable event
(Gold on a stricken column leafed like pollen)
Has offered my marrow and the gristle in my eye
To speculation, to a gaze that gluts its pallor
Airily, as after the Capitol had fallen
Aura of eagles fed on the foolish valour
Of abandoned mercenaries. Posthumous I am already
And suck sustenance from shapes provisional,
My own and others. Past, present, future
Feed a cool, abstracted stare

121

So that when comes smiling up beneath
Me a despatch-rider with a twist of grapes in his teeth
I am uncertain who it is — another
Or myself? — that brings me a lost message from my youth

With flute-music,
Flute-music to trickle upward like a vine
Divine a crevice in the uncorniced skies
And, with Dionysus sailing, civilize
The waste places merciless. Over the voiced
And fluted waves with flutes and soft recorders
Blown, fruition that blooms around elected action
Will cultivate the barbarous heavens with thin scions
Of a blossoming fiction,
Twine in the sky a trembling wake of spring.

AN EFFECT OF ILLUMINATION

A peacock train of stars along the water-stairs
Of the castled hill;
And the mild eye, innocent of its destiny,
Pale swimmer through blue, planetary light
Now lips the lymph and milky dream of heaven,
Plucks meteors idly like thin, golden threads
That rustle through the lapis lazuli,
Through shot-silk over silent, velvet water.
But those low, lion winks awakening the horizon ... ?
O innocent and distant, chime harmless as
The toll of patiently revolving bell-buoys.

Then systole of sky. Stillness become
A lion's den.
Wild meteors falling in our laps. Flames.
Dragonish flames and cries that call for breath.
The sphinctered sky seals off a livid bell-jar
On humiliated animals lost in holes. . . .
O mother! mother! cord to the mothering earth!
Our hearts run dry; our blood sucked downward
Through a straight, stretched tube, dangerously thin
And twanging breaks... breaks... How can it hold?
Pluck close this nested bird with brittle bones
A little longer. Receive it. Give it suck.
Exhausted vacuum below pulsating ribs,
Easy to crush as wrens' bones or a blown
Bird's egg, protect with vascular affection;
Protect, great mother, your exhausted sons.

And slowly through parched veins blood creeps again.
The world is wide and many are alive,
Delicately dawn will come with a garland of headlines –
But not to sensitive retinas damaged.
Thoughts, dreams, mild exhalations of the blood,

The amorous glance that anchors in wide air
The solitary heart are burnt, are blasted.
Knowledge, burst prematurely in the brain,
Peeled back time's barrel like a celery stalk
To show a cyclopean eye of quartz
That stared and blazed and blinded speculation.
Yes, heaven rebuilds its lavish masonry
But not for those whom battle has trepanned.
For shades who ruin with an opened skull
Night reigns perpetually in broad day,
Maleficent peacock with a thousand eyes of stone.

THE NEW VINTAGE

Wine of the new vintage they brought us
Bitter but the best they had
And by the wine or their kindness translated back to men,
Un-Circëd, we sat at ease in a spell of daylight
That we knew could never last. Though it did.
Day after day through amber richness dawdling
We hardly noticed the thin trickle of acidity
As one sun-caverned green-glass flask succeeded another
And the battle moved further away. It was an autumn solstice
Where we lay forgotten to play with children
In a vine-blessed house, a beatitude of husbandry
Discussing with the farmer crops and legends;
And returning rarely to our own sour dispensation
When tending the vehicles that sulked under leafy nettings.

Sons we were
Re-entered into a patrimony from which
Many of our fathers, grandfathers even, had been dispossessed.
And we moved through the house discovering family heirlooms,
Shocks of Indian corn that blazed from the rafters
And above the stairway tomatoes skeined in ruby clusters;
Or gazed through windows at fields and furrows
Where a woman switched on two milk-white oxen
Through bare fruit-trees, blue with copper sulphate,
That offered to the bare, blue sky fruits of repentance.
These things like the word of life we handled then.

But there is not a happy ending.
(Nor in the parable is mention made
Of the morning when the prodigal, redeemed and feasted,
Was sought in vain, once more a prey to bestial craving;
When his father found only a robe and mocking ring.)
One morning a signal came and in half an hour
We had loaded the vehicles and tied on extra gear,

Enough to make us at home in the winds and smoke
Where we would be coiled like wraiths through a new campaign.
We took the farmer's address and promised to write
And as he poured out the final viaticum
The new wine in our lying throats stung sharp and bitter,
There was no ray left of its sun-burnt, august sweetness.

He watched us to the last from the middle of the road
Staring along that barren tunnel as though down a rifle-barrel
Where the rifling circled in a glassy, baffling pool
Too deep with future for his aching temples,
A leaden pool that sucked down to he knew not what,
And shimmered with unheard-of consummations sterile.

THE PEACOCK

What was it on the midnight cried
In the lapsed garden of green solitude?
A strangled sob of grief escaping
The bronze-green throat of the bird of pride.

Armoured beneath its glossy side
Lost paradise is darkly hidden.
Only at midnight and alone
Can the brave, bronze coat divide.

Issue of tears that have never dried
Start from the wound in an anguished flow.
Through gardens shadowed by a sword
Echoes the pain that has never died.

I slept no more, no more denied
The fissure in my own proud nature –
To find at dawn a midnight feather
Pallor of grass had dignified.

Who in the lull is standing by my side
Speaking sub-audibly, a misted stream?
Someone I only half-know, muffled from me —
Murmurs to me or to advancing night
Or to himself? He has accomplished prodigies, I know,
Image of bronze rigidity, round which
The battle swirled. Can bronze lips speak
Or bronze lids fall? And I am lifted from my lethargy
However shamefully fallen, who long ago
Lived haunted by the hero and the river.
The stream articulates, obliterates destruction
Bears to me torn memorials, dismembered limbs.
His low words float the memory of his friend
Living but parted from the battle under shame,
His honour parcelled on the effacing flood.
Fragments I catch — fair hair, a stammer, weakness —
That would be hurried to oblivion
But for afflicted strength. Strength stoops and saves
Unequal honour from the waves. See
In a nimbus of love the drowning limbs reformed
Shine with original brightness. One mighty heart
Smoothes round his stain the resurrected light
And gives him back his differenced coat.

> *Sweet hope come home again! Night-floated dream*
> *Loosed from the wounded statue's side*
> *Resume with catching throat the silenced theme.*
> *To the meanest of the thrush's subjects*
> *Bear aromatic pledges of the crushed heart's vigour*
> *Bruised leaves, bruised petals pluck from the yawning stream.*

A black cloud folds me, and I am hallowed back
To my own authentic wood. Swirled manes ramp past,
Crescendo of needled boughs, bewilderment

Of darkness piped with crimson. What does the black
Flood offer, the night wood form? No voice or face.
Lost gestures becalmed in moving theatrical air. . . .
Close voiceless lips . . . hair where perfection tangles.
Sealed, silent statue that I know is breathing
See! I come through the dark with a flower in my hand
To seek you. Let the heavens be slashed and flushed with rose
And shadows memory-haunted as I approach
O unapproachable! Stone myths and urns
Be irised with the necks of dying peacocks
And the pierced thrush sing silvering all night long
Dark inlets of invisible desire.
Estranged from me — but yet you are not strange.
I see humanity as the wound you bear
Cleft in your side and mine uniting us
Where flower proud tissues of lasting isolation,
Dread posthumous flowers of our first hopes;
Till the troubled air buds, breaks and folds about me.
A banished rapture intervenes
As armadas of crimson flakes take wing
In rooted, deathless odysseys,
Everywhere held and spreading — into the heaven
Of a world reclaimed, caught up in the loose stanzas of love.

> *Rose, rose of the winds, here recompose*
> *In an integrity of suffering.*
> *Bring home the note of the exiled bird.*
> *With strains to heal incisions they expose*
> *Graft to the heart the thorn of the torn lyric.*
> *In the heart of the wilderness, O reassemble the rose.*

But what the blood has made fades, vanishes.
Flares fade and go out. On the splattered battlefield,
As the stranger vanishes, the infinity
Of finite solitudes resume their vigil,
Intricate thickets that the times would suck
Back to the slime and the age of monsters.
Mastodon and dinosaur could muzzle here

In this valley's slough, bats be regaled
In an ambiguity of blindly mated elements
With a species preying on itself — a trackless horror.
Yet as the scavenging eagle hangs and hovers
Escapes from its claws in tatters invincible song.
The torn heart can pour forth sweetness, and solitude
Extend ecumenical leaves and petals
In dark communion. Rapture of crimson
That streams from longer wars and deeper scars
Trembles behind the darkness, savour of light
That could bind a thousand scattered wounds, tender
As famished lips, in an artifact of tissue.
From the battle's catacombs to the cupola of heaven,
Where all the twitterings of love are gathered,
Springs the invisible rose through desolation,
Springs in a context of darkness
The rivelled gauze and gleam — and waits
To mediate like music between reality and dream.

THE NIMBUS

To dive for the nimbus on the sea-floor
    Or seek it in the sun
Calls for a plucky steeplejack
    Scaling sky's giddy ocean
Or dolphin-hearted journeyman
To swim from the foundered sunburst's roar
    With lost treasure on his back.

Ocean that slovens and sidles in vast
    Indifference, hides
In its sludge a wreath of drowning bells.
    Who in those tricky tides
Or up the slippery daybreak's sides
Can grapple the spices of morning fast
    That waste on the listless swells?

Smothered beneath a lowering ceiling
    All cock-crow crispness dies.
Bleary hordes are afraid to wake
    Into the mists that rise
From a palsied swamp where a marsh-bird cries.
Stranger, reconquer the source of feeling
    For an anxious people's sake.

Plunder the mind's aerial cages
    Or the heart's deep catacombs.
O daring's virtuoso, tossed
    Where the furious sunlight foams
Or through the instinct's twilit glooms,
Return with the sunburst's glistering pledges
    As a garland for the lost.

A bittern rusting in the reeds
    Is startled, and through the mist

Whirs screaming. Now, if now only, come
    With the nimbus in your fist.
Strike, strike the rust like a rhapsodist
And burnish gold each throat that pleads
    For dawn's encomium.

Outwitting waves would be no miracle tonight,

The waters are so calm. No god's rare gift
Of stable footing on the opening sea,
No sandalled glister for the enchanted drift,
Bind on; trust in the gulls' simplicity.

Folded, impervious, at peace they rest
As though this lustrous treachery were their home.
And safely they could build far out. A nest
Would live for months, twisted from tufts of foam.

Their breasts against the breathing of the deep
Are mild clouds in a sky of constant weather.
And so the sky on this ambiguous sleep
Glides down, falls like a blue king-fisher's feather.

For seas are skies and skies are seas, where float
Cool swansdown clouds that sundown has subdued.
Shadowed the snow about a swan's white throat;
The daylight melts; slowly they drift and brood.

How dim that far horizon, those wan cries!
Where bone to water turns, bright flesh to air.
The shadows circling in the glassy twilight
Cry out for company on the trailing stair,

Where following them would be no miracle tonight.

Lack-lustre now the landscape, too long acquainted
With death and wounds. Only the orchard where
Persimmons smoulder in the darkening air,
Like cressets guttering to an orange glow,
Preserves the landscape the old masters painted;
A glimmer in green leaves and glossy bark,
A radiance rescued from the pouring dark,
A fragment of the glister of Uccello.

Through that green secrecy my limbs would drown
Drifting enfranchised down a still bay, preened
By art, a peacock lustre damascened
With meandering dreams and pleasures, where unconstrued
Would waters hide me with their amaranth crown.
Even the fishermen who fish night-long
With flares would never net my rapturous song,
Leafy with marvels like a romantic wood.

Pleasure? A romantic wood? The other trees
Have felt the venom of a senseless flail
And on the threshing-floor are dying, pale
As wounded men on whom the darkness hardens.
The farm is pock-marked with a strange disease.
The craters suppurate an acid sea
That, spreading, blots out old calligraphy.
A peasant points and says, "These all were gardens."

No. I cannot from a few leaves twist
A sheltering chaplet even of despair,
When trees and fields for miles around are bare.
If there is any comfort, then I must find
It in the open where the dead insist
How cold the earth has turned. This lingering swoon

Of colour is ambushed fatally, and soon
The fruit will fall like kings in a rebel wind.

O entropy that has involved our hearts!
A mother kindles withered twigs beneath
A pot and lets them die for lack of breath.
The farmer risks the dull, gun-metalled sky
And, slouching barefoot through the shell holes, starts
To shave more fodder from the dripping straw-stack,
Forgets his purpose and comes empty-handed back.
The age is guttering to senility.

But she (the woman who is my wisdom) writes
That every age has been faint-hearted, redeemed
By daring horsemen, whose gold stirrups gleamed
On the flanks of the lathered time, past the dark croup
Spattering brightness; and their extreme delights —
Turmoil, difficulty and a distant quarry —
Were frescoed as the background of their glory.
And I believe her — but hear no huntsmen up.

The soldiers, huddled in the night's neglect,
Know only that the weather here has broken,
Deep in their bones the coming snow has spoken
Death. With lonely men in the moon's eye
I stare at ruts and puddles that reflect
Clay-tarnished splendour and, in the doom of words,
Nail to my shuttered heart with pitted swords
The weather, exile and man's agony.

Brave salamander, bring me back delight,
Flame's darling in desired extremity!
Break the crisp meal of fire for me to share
Suck me wild honey from the pollen-bright
And tyrannous truculence
Of the sun's bearded glare
That from defeated violence
Smeared with the sweetness of necessity
I may escape into all-cloistering air.

Lodge on my sleeve as on a battlement.
I am a dungeon, the colour of a castle,
Where my heart lies galled, galled by a lost crusade.
The dark keep hides no crust of nourishment,
Furious the sun. O crumble
It to bread! Then lead
Me past the curtain-wall till humble
As a friar I become the sky's own vassal
And go triumphant, blessing its barbarous shade.

Archaic creature, I would wear you chevroned
On my arm as emblem of a naked heart.
Bare must I trudge — with you my minister —
To be by desert wanderings saracened.
If you who in noon's fire
Can savour peace like myrrh
Will with sweet sinewy tongue inspire
Me forth, I yet may fill a soldier's part,
I yet may see the Holy Sepulchre.

Grey as a wasp's nest swinging in the wind.
An old man. Too old an empty vessel to visit
With the venom of so many uncommitted sins.
Tears had sieved his brains to conduits
Where desires that fell as hatred on his head
Were sluiced away. He had outlasted his grief.
Who had been so monstrously hurt — and his eyes put out —
Had no more tears to weep; but would not die.
Unreason's residue in the grey dusk unsublimed.

A pariah to the dogs; to children
A rotten maypole for fear to frolic round;
To all citizens of substance, an obscene offence
Since his wax head could twitch the cerements from the grave
Of lavish, foolish things that they had buried,
Evolve in twilight grey labyrinths of regret.
And to himself? He still remembered when he had been
More than a mock for children or a blasted oak
To stand the sensuous shock of hate
From other men's impossible desires,
More than an excuse for failed crops and luckless love-affairs.

His brain had been a high urn filled with flowers.
"Recant. Recant and die," the failing light insisted.
But he would fumble: "Let other hands unweave the dead
Flowers' ghostly web. I will await the ultimate end
In a sepulchre of memories.
Whose flesh once bore the rainbow's flash
May not deflower his triumph's cenotaph."
And, hour after hour, would twist, untwist, blanched colours
Of the bow that broke beneath the avalanche.

Then one day the stalk of his sorrow struck root.
Sweetness welled in the desert, he felt his dry

137

Brains swelled with light, wafer of honeyed light
That he would break in showers for the world to share;
And kindness dripping from his finger-tips like milk.
First of his foes, the dogs, snuffed change and, fawning,
Began to lick his sores, with pity first
But soon adoring. Then children secretly
Took benediction from his withered hands.
Till at length the wrongs he had suffered, or his crimes,
(For had they been wrongs or crimes?)
Were subtly reassessed, reversed, forgotten.
Now, sanctioned by the magistrates, the young –
Whose bright limbs he may never see or touch –
Bask in his light of blinded concentration
And, the troubles of their budding passions stilled,
Hear in his head the beehive roar of the sun.

It was through a mucous membrane, a kind of mouth
Most tender to the touch, that dreamily
I swam into my own sick-room, south
Of this tropic, in a soft wind, a lymphatic sea.

Lying on the bed as though flayed
And stretched in an anatomical chart, muscles
Cross-hatched with nerves to the shamed air splayed
Rant as red as a cock's comb. Around me rustles

Translucent drapery disposed in a paper-thin
Illusion of late afternoon, a bland and blond
Stockade that stems the murk it dabbles in,
Though slimed like film where a serpent brood is spawned.

What was it made ensanguined fury cease?
By the bed two animals arrested stand,
A lion holding up a blood-stained fleece
And a leopard with an hour-glass in its hand.

Gold has been blown into the air. As the onset waned
Gold fleeced from the flesh and gold from the sliding hour
Have branched in the air and stiffened. Was it this restrained
The scathing lion and tranced the leopard's power?

But daylight darkens into deep gold, dark gold, black.
As the pale stockade is overwhelmed, I know
Red craving after one more night attack
Would be devoured — or left for flies to blow.

Then comes a lady in the failing light
With black lawn over sheerest, golden tissue,

Unknown where she comes from, daughter of night,
And like the beasts one of the shadows' issue.

Gliding from nowhere in the dying truce
Her gaze above the red flayed patient dwells,
A gaze of mildness, of the flower-de-luce,
That hovering, treats with savagery, compels

To mildness lecherous tongues impatiently lolling.
She soothes the lion and the leopard calms.
Now both are feeding as the dew is falling,
Lapping contentment from her milk-white palms.

And ravening tongues now moonily caress
The form they butchered; now gentled, salve and save;
The stars their lost dominions repossess.
Again in fleecy skies the lilies wave.

If in the ear the lizarding summer
Were to set up its audience-chamber of gold and stubble
Hung all year long with tissue of clear azure
Painting the tympanum with steeples of red clover
Where sleepy bells nod to the circling bees. . . .
If in the chambers of the eye
Slow blue seleucid ages could constantly
Be couched and cushioned, in splendour coffered and recessed
To receive proud embassies of far and facile clouds,
Winds wafting them and trees obsequious. . . .
If all the brain's most secret passages,
Bays and dry lagoons, byzantine labyrinths,
With honeysuckle flooded and the breath of clover
Should float, like wayward nymphs,
Gondola-sails of dragon-flies, damsel-flies. . . .
In the profusion of roses, breezes, gala odours
Reason would its dividing crown renounce
Sink in the commonwealth of sense
And with the watery flesh be wedded, the golden orb
Along the branching veins dissolving run
Till pollened limbs, with the energy of animals
And thought of angels, be reunited with the sun.

A MAN OF HONOUR

When he awakened to himself, it was
Perpetual day. He must go on beneath
The midnight sun that hung its icy laws
Rebukingly about him, purging his breath.
Sharp lookout must be kept. No slackened pause
To sleep, no night to sip one drop of death.

Silently as an Arctic convoy steers
He must be stern and lonely, from the raked wings
Of his patrolling vices hide his fears.
At action stations always. One false move brings
A pack of submarines, one whimper tears
The tissued pallor where salvation sings.

Round many a crackling North Cape must he pass
Estranged from land, long centuries move
Snow-blinded, bewildered by the hectic compass,
Till at the valid pole at last arrive
His bearded honour frozen green as grass
And ashen eyes the sun burnt out, alive.

IN A SPRING NIGHT

Troubled the tree when spring returns.
Into the dark, ancestral wood
Renascence wakening, is ghosted with whiteness.
Shadows withdraw, lost radiance burns.
But the strength that many months withstood
Cruel snows can hardly bear such lightness,
Deftness. At the torched, triumphant budding
Gorged boughs ache earthward with foreboding:

Remembering how in other springs
Impassioned streams through dry veins crept,
Unlocked reluctant doors, unfroze
Black roots to airy carollings,
As the fatal, feckless currents swept
Past all measure; how at the close –
O heartbreak! Crimson agony! –
Those deaths still live in the death-pale tree.

I

How villainous the empty wine-vats grow
Here in the candlelight as I wait for fire-orders,
How cloaked and felted with shadows. The brown and bat-
Winged air has thickened to a brackish silence,
Brimming over old rakes and harness in the corner,
Filling the empty stalls, gathering and settling,
Swung from the storm on the gimbals of an ancient house.
So melancholy-still it is, so distant seems
The wash of shell-fire overhead, I hear
Adrift in the squandered grain the discourse of mice
Like filaments strung through this clouded calm,
Think I can even hear the cellar-spiders
Tugging from their guts their viscous webs.
I am the only other animal awake.
No messages. No new intelligence
Conducted to the low-plucked gloom unriddles
The suspense or signals changing weather;
Superior to clumsy hands, the fire-program
Continues, the shells interweaving, theirs and ours
In a maze of literal madness. The lines are quiet.
But in the smother something strains to speak.
In the clammy touch that wakes my throat there is
Entreaty, is entrance of an amnestied familiar,
Summons and recognition from a withering hand.
Commingled in the air the sweat and sighs
Of fifteen soldiers sleeping withers and grieves
About me. Exiled. Sour with the taint of exile.
Sour with the taint of surfeit. The heavy breath
Of men who have gorged all day on fear and danger,
Have supped with devils, dabbled in stews of corruption.
I smell the crooked nomadic ways they came.

144

II

Cut-throats, the shadows lead me with black knives
To vulnerable flesh. There the argument continues,
Lost seigneuries of childhood in wilderness
Engulfed, limbs gross with the leaves of darkness, and vines
Infesting the ruined chapel. My eyeballs are
Skewered forward to hang peering, shuddering. How far
The settlements are recessed! the candle almost out!
One of the sleepers moving in his sleep
Is tangled in a mess of gear, and groans;
One shows his back as brown as a tobacco leaf;
One sighs; one lies as though his neck were broken.

Dim spires far down the rapid river.

After the festivals of savagery (loud bodies
Writhing with vermilion), after flares and flames
And the stare of madness — this stupor of leather,
Where derangement of the subtlest tissues, still
Smouldering, creeps underground; and the breath
Of the burning bark, that innocence encased
And faggoted, seduces still in absence.
After the long traverse. The mind sunk sceptreless
In flesh till heat, cold, hunger, pain
As tetrarchs reigned, arbitrary usurpers.
After the ultimate rapids where the cargo was lightened,
The white caesura that stripped down longings
To the compass of these serviceable packs of greasy memories,
At the white mist where finally faded the bells —

Bells break the joists of swaying towers.

This rest in the meagre feast of deep necessity:
Grain spilled on the floor, the empty wine-vats, dirty straw,
Enthusiasts and thieves together lying
Awkwardly in a bare thieves' kitchen.
Ache down, my eyes, along the closing vista

145

From prodigals and children pell-mell scattered
Through the choked pores and rivers, the paths blood-speckled,
Where animals fought infatuate and leaves
Are waiting for rain, to the shrunk estuary
By spires and settlements surrounded . . . so distant!
The bay spread small and smooth as milk, a seed
Of cloud troubling the savage voyagers,
Trouble of birth in the winter-strangled tree
That can flower again and again through embarrassed bark
With buds and bells beclouded.

Bells buried in the earth and broken.

Leaves cursed with blood, voluptuous fronds of darkness,
O aboriginal heaviness in which
My gaze is limed and exiled! The wilderness
Laocoöns this ancient settlement.
Rusts and broods by the wall the heavy mattock,
The sickle tarnishes. And the husbandmen,
Cast out to see what wisdom there may be
In husks, stumble through trip-wires. If I should find
An emblem of order, a scythe that year after year
Mooned through the grass, disparaged it is
By shadows, in feverish growth sick metal sweats.
Or caves where the heart of the sleeping wine was warmed
And the sunburnt melody of summer extended
As a link in the seemingly endless garland of harvests,
They are gutted those caves, and hollow as gourds.
The song of the seasons is broken, the diadem
Star-studded, revolving in patient ecstasy
Over bent backs and rotated furrows, cracked.

Down fading spires stars trickle out.

The guns have shaken the stars from their sockets,
The weeping certainties of generation, cracked,
The voice of consolation, cracked.
Tonight the wilderness is here and everywhere.

And here sluggishly drifting (but seined by my candle
That sails mildly fishing through the dark)
Welters a gentle crew. Mangered in unease,
By sombre streams reduced, stripped naked,
Relation leaves them and identity,
Though childhood still is lilied in closed lids.
Dim to me

                      Dim spires far down the rapid river.

              eyelids that fleur-de-lis the dark
Impeach the absent stars. O much traduced
And tarnished flesh, where guns and hungers peal,
Abandoned here beneath the blow of history,
But silvered still and still imperial
In the phosphored wash what quick life starts,
What filaments are spawned from misery?

III

Awake and conscious, and god-like so.
But the impotent god of a lost creation.
To pacify this brawl of whispers
My breath goes from me, and is impotent.

Spirits that weave the petals of the weeping flowers
Speak for me, speak natural powers,
While at the base of my brain
An ampoule of pity
Swells like a trillium.
Would break, would break in a cedar breath
From untarnished lakes and rivers,
Lakes of sweet water, skies of unsullied godhead.
Would suck in through the blanket at the door
Fresh breezes to this fetid lair
To wash all trace of cordite from the air.

147

Enters, though, as the blanket stirs aside
The scent of death, the sentinel,
Scent of dead horses and dead men,
O sickly sweet! The scent of nitre.

If there were stars and skies accessible,
A brightly tented system to bless
And diadem them whole like glistening hills at evening...
If there were heavens to call to,
A promontory of comfort, some peak of comprehension...
But dark, dark.

Guards of the house:
A dead horse with turds half-bulging from its rump,
A sergeant dead in the ditch, half-buried,
Green as his tunic. Verdigris blots him.
The whites of his eyes are scrawled with flies,
The hair of his head now dead and excremental.
These termini of nature picketing the nether pit
Impose a stern perimeter,
Guard the thick ferment, thought-threaded nakedness,
Clouding the fallible, fallen star in its own brightness,

In gusts redound on my diminished light
With foul air reeking, and send me back defeated.

IV

Absorbed. Given over to their silence. A membrane listening.
Misery is moving like the mother in a liquid.
"What will become of me?" Wash of the wilderness
Folds a thin filament, a white dissected nerve
In isolation. "How like a knife in my guts
His glance has stayed." Hangs in the air a moment
That cry, a dagger, slits open my ear. Thin fronds
Sharpened by scalpels sway in the brown bat-light.
Flesh has been cut by leaves of bitter laurel,

Tissue been cut away and the sheaths of brightness,
Environing lymph lapped up by fire
Till insidious fibres twitch their charged message
Nakedly, publish their lamentation. "Lost.
O something that I lost as I was wandering."
Struggling in the consistory of silence
To clothe their fallen anonymity
These limbs now never to be free from lesion
Cry through white nerves, cry seeking themselves
In a nameless ferment. Strand after strand I hear,
Phrase after phrase blown one way by the muffled wind.
And so the air is peopled. One breathes, "I've seen too much."
Another, "Let me be lucky and be killed."
These threads and hairs combed into a theme of nerves
Paint with so fine a brush the tympanum
Of a temple where the divinity is dying
I think of trees that sigh as the night wind rises
Of boughs lifting, quivering, green and black and grey
As bats and night-hawks pluck the sky's stretched membrane.
A theme of nerves, a downward branching tree
Where single fibres snap and link, are joined
In a system downwards, misery to misery linked,
Are interlaced in a light and delicate embrace.
These whispers harp to a proud king softly.
Joined . . . joined . . . joined in a tree of animal
Heaviness, of animal kindness.
I hear the sighing of a dark green tree.
White filaments compose a live green tree.
O I have listened long enough! My brain
Runs ruining down the desired descent, descent
Desired and paid for, down to the weedy dungeon
Where their cries are prisoned, where their breath is mist,
Where I myself am lying. Their cries are mine,
Their miseries thrill through my impoverished nerves,
People the dungeon of my bowels with fancies.
These are my villain fancies also.
No others would I have as my familiars,
No other company than this. In the ooze

149

And reeking vapours of a barren cellar,
I would have only such still and subterranean music,
Blind fingering of mice through destitution
And spidery tentacles as a covering for the brain,
A kind of comfort. Beneath a crumbling house
I sift the detritus of dreams with a goodly company.
In the heart-sick earth these clammy manacles,
These tendrils straggling in a turbid stream
Are furnishing enough as the night wind rises.
Rises to a muffled roar as the nearest guns
Resume methodical vituperation,
The whole house wheezing like a bellows,
And imprisoned tendrils, lifting, blowing all one way.

V

The candle starts and flickers
Interrogates the shadows, leaves them still more secret
The candle of the lord gone over to the captive voices
Enfolded in foul air,
Unkinged, uncrowned, and minion now
To every gust that blows the spider's wreckage.

Still the slow spider weaves.
And so make to trial. To imitate the spider,
From our unravelled tissues,
To spin an intellectual thread, no more
Mercurial nor more pure than this so precious crew,
That mounting, mounting, breaking, respun, as thin
As starlight, perhaps at last might clasp the upper air
And there restore relation and identity.
With webs dilating in lucid dialectic
Might jewel and justify limbs weak as gossamer,
Perhaps with eloquence of stars might stud
The drift of animal affection, and so make fast
A habitation in the wilderness.

Perhaps.
        But thick dew falls on my face.
I am gummed all over with a strange balsam.
I am sticky with sweat and with humankind
That fastens and laces me here. I am content.
Here is my place in a friendly heaven for a night
Where they have built a word- and star-less system
Perfectly. Our sighs like the milk
Of the milky way arch over us. Corrupted
Our lungs breathe out a new heaven of pity and concern.

DAYBREAK

On this rock landed from love's lunar sea
He marvels how the grinding waves have ceased,
And the virginal sky, cloud-craftily curling,
Is unicorned with gratuitous gems.
Of the ocean's shaggy rapture
Nothing is left but a trace of froth and frippery.
Light on the pine-tree tops is tangled airily
Thrust like sonnets on the tiara of his paramour.

SOMETHING STILL TO FIND

THE GREEN MAN

Leaves twist out of his mouth, of his eyes, of his ears,
twine down over his thighs, spring out of his heels,
as he runs through the woods as a deer or an outlaw, or curled
up in moss and bracken, light speckling him feckless,
he watches the other animals, himself hidden
like an animal, although so strangely human
that if you surprise him you might think yourself looking
into the eyes of the mad but all-wise Merlin.

Boreal forest his most natural habitat
from the edge of our cities up to the tree-line
where at summer's end in the spongy Mackenzie Delta
he glides through pale yellowing poplars before the snow flies
or at Northwest River slips out of the spruce to play
with the huskies, chained on the shingle. His territory
spreads far and wide beneath the Bear. Morose
and frolic and savage his sports where the forests are.

But I have glimpsed him almost everywhere.
In pool-rooms and bargain-basements. In the glance of the dark
prisoner in the dock, not knowing how to plead,
passionate the criss-cross light that sifts through leaves.
In pale changing-rooms at the atomic energy plant
the young technician is changed into a sylvan man,
shadowed with mystery, and suffering from the sap
like a young green tree, quick thrall of earth and frenzy.

And quick he runs through my dreams, so quick and grieving,
to banish grey calculations of tomorrow,
to banish old gods with gay assurance,
impatient of bounds and all mere definition,
but sometimes himself a god, now minor, marginal,
now reigning sovereign over an empty tomb,

the incised leaves on his flesh now wounds, now blood,
now flame. The forest reeks now with vermilion.

There is a shade that glides beneath the skyscrapers
and makes those papery steeples soar and tremble
like poplars in the breeze, a green man's shade
who came before Champlain, green traveller, trader,
debauchee, wearing around his neck
gull's feathers and four new sweetwater seas,
interpreting the woods to Europe and Europe to
the woods — till finally he was cooked and eaten.

His taciturnities were our title-deeds,
his heart divided food that our hearts have fed on,
so many morsels from that seething pot,
some for the merchant princes in their lofty
boardrooms (a long long way from poor Etienne Brulé!),
but more for more ravenous hunters through other wastes,
lost, lost, and wild in utter inner dark
where the hunters and the circling hunted are the same.

And so I circle on the green man's tracks,
allured, bewildered by the bright green shoots
and headsman's axe he holds, those baffling icons
(for all the subtle theories that I half believe in)
that lead me on and down. But past all doubt
there thrives an underworld where life and death
are woven. And it is bright and dark and savage,
as speckled and as rippling as a snakeskin.

Outlaw or god this cunning harlequin?
I feel him darkening my glittering veins,
he kennels in my loins, knows every crevice
of my half-breed heart, and yet eludes me still,
though rumours reach me of him fugitive,
laughing and drinking behind an empty warehouse,

156

disguised in rags, and tossing empty bottles
to splash and sparkle on the cindery railway-siding.

Scion of the undergrowth and underworld
but a prince of darkness in all daylight polity.
I could lead you on a perfect summer afternoon
into a clearing where the trees are still and lucid
and have you stare and listen till a rustle comes
of a serpent moving underneath the columns.
Light slows. Leaves tremble — with Marsyas' blood as much
as Apollo's brightness. Now break a branch, it bleeds.

Some nights and seasons are his own, and sacred.
Then dreams flow into the woods, woods flow
into dreams, the whole pent city dreaming of a carnal
wood, confluence that empties into the streets
with a scurry of leaves and carnival drums and flutes,
and torches that set fire to the leaves and the city, a blaze
of harlequin crimson, skyward, as quick he still winds
among the masquers mocking, a green man with green wounds.

Suddenly he stopped running.
The air was breathless, spiked with thorn,
oak-leaves rattling from dead branches,
the scene so ruinous
a king's crown might have been found on a bush.

All he could feel was cold and pain.
Touch he had discarded like an empty cartouche-
box. For a while he could hear the angry owl,
but now not that, nothing.
Cold had burned him down to the bone.

He stood stock-still, like a skeleton, waiting.
Where were all his companions?
the lovely disguises that had deserted him one by one
since the *sauve-qui-peut* and the terrible rout.
Could they ever rejoin him as stragglers?

They had left him — his crimson sensual coat,
his suit of leaves like a man from the woods,
even the rich filigree of nerves —
left him. . . . Or had he left *them*?
given them up as alms to the wolves?

He didn't know. He was waiting.
Then like caribou over the tundra
came shambling the rags of a former richness:
a coat that once had been sleek and scarlet
but weatherbeaten now, torn, tattered

and folding itself against the cold;
and another disguise in dull rifle green
that seemed to be full of menace,

seemed now a spirit of destruction only
shorn of its old wild ambiguity.

They wouldn't approach too close,
these and other familiar wraiths,
but hung in the air like gaunt ruins
of a wardrobe. And he was powerless
to call or summon.

But the air seemed suddenly milder.
If a bird should sing
or a breeze breathe lightly over his hand
a word might come that would allow them to sign
a sorrowful injured concordat.

Tower in the throat
now turned to ice
where nothing now can pass
no breath sound song
gorged with lost paradise
torn tissues stiffening freezing
 O my lost kingdom!

There had been birds
in a bright pavilion
and breathless breath and words
that he remembered half-remembered
light snowdrifts misting blue mountains
tissues of dalliance
 O my lost kingdom!

Bell in the tower
fallen into the pit
a bell as heavy as lead
swings drunkenly for the dead
as mist fades and loved ghost leaves
on its final outward transit
 O my lost kingdom!

Dreams strong in death
break continents
slit starry tents to ribbons
sharp passage of a blood-blown thing
cuts orbs and heavens down
to tangle in blood-shot grass
 O my lost kingdom!

Now sways a gallows
in place of the tower
where the furred imperial tongue
babbles of pleasures gone
tongue dissolute with tears
its sinewy strength undone
    O my lost kingdom!

Till in wild grass
in wilderness
hair matted drenched with dew
he nuzzles on all fours
a hungry haunted animal
licking up blood and tears
    O my lost kingdom!

O apple apple of a thousand tongues
    sing from the bough in dolour
for a thousand wounds that will not heal
    and lips drained dry of colour.

So many wounds so many sighs
    such muffled suffering
so many unfilled pleas outstretched
    where you sway glittering.

This autumn evening I have seen
    you rise through leaves and fires
into pure air where godhead gathers
    and hungers and desires

that feed you daily with their wants
    and bring you radiance
O far from closing boughs and vines
    O life-in-death of distance.

How with your cheeks the winds are charred
    winds of eternal autumn
that gleam with fruit unharvested
    long after harvest-home.

I stand within your plenitude
    as in a sacred grove.
The shrewd winds strip my cravings bare
    forbidding me to move

till I have prayed for other shades
    that taste this sweet-shrewd savour.
Your godhead gathers from their wounds.
    Look down this night with favour.

O apple apple of a thousand tongues
    sing from the bough in dolour
send out a pentecost of flames
    to hallow the grieving air.

THE DOUBLE

Love, I laid my love away
        far so far
to return some other day
but the rains came and the snows
now as the searching north wind blows
I scrabble in vain under leafless trees.

I kept trinkets in a drawer
        dark so dark
a pistol and a single tear
three words of magic cased in air.
Who was it came and forced the lock?
Who will give me my treasures back?

I have a double who looks like me
        like so like
I wonder I wonder if it was he
who filched my love when I was gone
rifling the cage where the dark sun shone
plundering with hands so like my own.

There is a light that comes from loss
        clear so clear.
Whatever it was a theft or loss
it's hard to pretend I was betrayed
since I was my double, I'm afraid,
and it was my heart that I mislaid.

HIDEOUT

He had shut all the windows and doors
and thrown away the keys
and sat in the cellar, stifling.

But the terrorists found him of course,
as he knew they would.
"All we want is one of your fingers.
No, not that one.
The one with the ring on it."
So he gave them that
and they chopped it off.

Then a peacock screamed.

They didn't know how far down he had fallen.

SEA-DREAM

I am stitched in coarse sail-cloth
a shroud covering me top to toe.

There are weights at my feet
I am heavy as lead.

The last stitch of the needle
has gone through my nostrils.
                                    I didn't cry out.

Now the plank is tipped seaward.

I lie rigid and dream
in the shark-shadowed waters.

BAREFOOT SAILORS

What are the new ships bringing,
    their white sails spread,
to me in my island kingdom
    as I wait in hope and dread?

Is their gift an innocent bride,
    infanta of maiden foam,
or contagion in the planking
    of punks from the stews at home?

I have heard of ships charged with gold
    as much as a king could spend.
But what if the glistering bullion
    were to prove fool's gold in the end?

Ships have brought treaties of peace
    and envoys with friendly words,
but others hide under their hatches
    culverins, muskets, swords.

In my dreams a ship is arriving
    with nothing more to declare
than two beautifully plumaged birds,
    two tanagers sleek and fair.

But my doubts and my dreams dissolve,
    the crew I have been waiting for lands.
Rough sailors mount the shingle
    with marlin-spikes in their hands.

SCENARIO FOR A LOVE-STORY

This will do as a sketch.

Have him summoned into the presence
and entertained there with lutes and sherbet.
Then at a sign from the prince
the curtains part
and two doctors come in and cut out his tongue.

"Now would you sing for me?"

But that makes no difference.

So a month later he is ushered in again,
again lutes and sweetmeats and satins.
Then the same cunning doctors cut off
his testicles, bowing, presenting them dutifully
on a silver paten.

"Now would you like to make love to me?"

But that makes no difference either, the slave is still
in love with the prince.

(And you can play it through reel after reel
only changing one sex, or the other, or both,
or the time, or the place, or the décor.
They'll all call it sick, sick, but they'll keep
coming back, don't ask me why.
It's sure to gross more than ten million.)

IN PLACE OF AN ELEGY

The taste won't leave my mouth
taste of his dying
alone in his house, by the lake
surrounded by pines and sumach.

The taste of it won't leave me
but keeps trickling into my mouth
drop after drop, of something bitter
clove or cinnamon or anise
or ooze from an abscess in my mouth.

He had so much to give, and gave so much
gave so much to me, and took so little
although he needed to take, and I to give
(bitterest of all that he could take so little)
bitter in my mouth
almost as taste of my own dying.

In my mouth the frost of pomegranate seeds
ice coloured with blood
freezing.

If I could, I would cut for him a stone
proud as his mountain in Montreal
looking out over the river, seaward,
or twist a wreath to hang in his woods
in memory of his foiled gentle heart
deep rich and generous (so gentle and generous to me).

I can't, though, I can't
the taste won't leave my mouth

taste of his dying
that mingles with mine
a taste so strong it might blow off my skull,
furious, like the furious blast from a shotgun.

THE MALCONTENT

Who could have dreamed another world
would open — and to a malcontent
who had frowned so many years away
beneath the eaves of a vanished perfection?

One hour of blossom and beginning
that fell so quietly from the bough,
and quickly, he hardly sensed its going
or guessed that loss could be so lasting.

And then long barren ages left
by dead honeysuckle and drifted cordite,
a leathery landscape which he knew
could never blossom more for him;

even when others saw pale buds
rejoin the bough in random ardour
he stood dismissed from joy. All
he smelt blindly was a stark dead tree.

His whole life now a fired perimeter
where he paced aimless as a sentry.
Faith having failed him once, he scorned
to trust in any living thing.

Perimeter of disappointment!
His eyes were visored by regret,
his cheeks sun-chapped and sabre-scarred,
his cap drawn guardsmanlike and low.

Half-hidden, his gaze was angry always
with the livid sky or treacherous earth,

angry, morose, and nonbelieving,
and ready always for the worst.

Till one morning he found creation changed,
with valentines on all the trees,
birds singing sweetly in their deft
bright coteries . . . the world transformed.

The whole world swinging orbed and sweet
like a kiss blown from a happy heart;
and all because of limbs bestowed
so freely in a night of thunder.

Perhaps it might not last, he knew that.
But never more could there return
despair of sand and sad surrender,
all the dire, sick savour of defeat.

Now there is a half-smile on his lips,
as he does whatever needs to be done.
Let the worst come. He wears his cap
at a new angle to the universe.

ASTROLABE

Now it seems almost as easy as breathing
this commerce of bodies and souls, unlicensed.
There was a moment, though, when it cost almost
everything — the explorer, tense, frightened, resolute,
with his cargo of musket, memories, diaries,
astrolabe, committing himself to the tender
skin of a birch-bark canoe, and a new continent,
and a new world, where anything might happen,
anything, not knowing that the thin skin of birch
might hold the weight of a lyric future
as well as the weight of suffering Europe on its ribs.
They grew to each other, though, slim lyric sweetness
and grim tension of the malcontent, till they
worked out new terms of trade, the musket
melting beside the pile of beaver pelts
till it rose again as a rod of almost god-like strength
and sweetness, and the pile of musky pelts flowered into
an ineffably golden fleece. At last the moment came when
he searched no longer for the stars, throwing away
his astrolabe to rust beneath a pine-tree,
and moved at last at ease in a world he never dreamed,
this new world, ours, where savagery and sweetness melt as one.

To the dark tower came, to the dark wood came,
and were frightened these children.
One said, "I'm still afraid of the dark." The other said nothing.
There should have been someone to guide them in
and there would have been — some dutiful page,
or wise old palmer, or peasant the colour of clay,
or perhaps a magical bird to fly
from the turret carrying a message —
if the land had been what the prologue promised.
But this was a blind bitter land, as most lands are.
There was no one. Darkness deep and forbidding.
Then one of them said to the other, "This is a wood
where we must find our own way,"
and put out his hand and parted the darkness.
In the morning so surely so safely they lay
in each other's arms in the leafy clearing
that birds flew out of the tower in blessing.

A CLUSTER OF LOVE POEMS

I

SONG

I was whipped, I was whipped
　　my brains were flayed
I was running like mad
　　as the searchlights played
till I came to myself in the dark of your arms
　　ah dancer, ah sweet dancer.

I was smashed, I was smashed
　　my bones were sore
I was ready to fall
　　I could stand no more
till I recovered my heart in the mesh of your mouth
　　ah dancer, ah sweet dancer.

I was bushed, I was bushed
　　I was dying alone
my blood had thickened
　　I was turned to stone
till I felt on my flesh the print of your limbs
　　ah dancer, ah sweet dancer.

I was crazed, I was crazed
　　as I looked out on the street
at the switch-blade faces
　　the trampling feet
I was poised on the edge when you swung me around
　　ah dancer, ah sweet dancer.

Now the sweet dance of bodies
　　given and taken
wide wash of nakedness

as we awaken
light lustrously, silkily, rippling between us
ah dancer, ah sweet dancer.

Lustrous and smooth
your lover's art
but strong as chain-mail
when we part
you, love, the armourer of my heart
ah dancer, ah sweet dancer.

LEAVES AND LYRICS

Leaves protect me, lyrics shade me
from the angry god who made me.
Birds skim down with songs to save me,
sing me back the strength god gave me.

Nature joins both power and loving,
strong sap's beating, leaves' soft moving,
fold me in your green caressing
twine your veins and mine in blessing.

You are nature's child and minion,
strong your arm as eagle's pinion,
tender leaves your membranes beating,
our flushed veins two natures meeting.

I am yours for your green sheathing,
strong because of your sweet breathing,
new restored by your achieving;
a dark flower opens past believing.

III

SECOND GROWTH

A power-line marching through scrub,
that's what you've made me.

A transmission tower
crackling with messages, images.

A sunflower
aching sunward with seed.

A stricken tree
blossoming into flower and fruit.

Old limbs
new baptized into youth.

Passion of
a saviour streaming with blood.

Strength of
a saviour in a sheer white cloth.

IV

EMBLEM

Wild orchid, veined with tenderness,
that reaches down to glacial rock
past moss and rotting ferns and pine-cones
and the droppings of porcupines, raccoons.

This your just signet, seal and impress,
a moccasin plant on granite growing,
pink in the sun-shot shade of June,
frail trumpet, satin-smooth, and clear.

A flower, so fragile, soon will fade.
But while it lasts its fine-meshed membrane
both holds and hides a veined perfection,
a slipper that a prince might search for.

This emblem of the sensitive
and strong, triumphant short-lived song —
for you this emblem will not fade
but blazoning be and heraldry.

V

AUBADE

Your name on my lips. Every night
as my eyes close. And the sweetness
of your body, as though you were with me.

Your name on my lips. Every morning,
waking, that one word on my lips.
I remember everything, everything.

But this morning there was nothing.
Then before I could think how strange it was
I was murmuring other words,

"Deeper than death or the dark,"
as though your mouth were on mine.
I love you that deeply, that deeply.

SEPTEMBER SUNLIGHT

It might almost be spring
the weather is so fine and lyric and sensual
with not a hint anywhere of decay or of dying,
bright, rather, with new faces setting off to classes
and rich with light cascading through green oak-leaves.

The air surrounds me like silk
as it twirls and untwirls (I might be a maypole)
in long gala streamers that attach me to you.
I turn in your direction, where you live now,
and feel on my face the faint glow of a sun-king.

I feel myself in the presence —
with the pride, at a distance, of a chosen favourite
who has yet to be fully acknowledged but whose face
has been brushed by the gold of secret election
like the gold of a moth's wing or of delicate sunburn.

Beyond the presence and palace
the markets are piled high with blue grapes
and with peaches as downy as the cheeks of epheboi.
Abundance floats in the air like a watermark,
I feel love from my fingertips dripping like milk.

He will dance at any door
for a wedding, funeral
or no reason at all,
priceless in catastrophe
(since then, of course, he gets no fee)
hop-sa-sa, with wild-fire hair
                     and lollipop stare
and a few poor jokes to crack
as the arrased flames swell ripe, real, rustling at his back.

Who now is masterless
and on the crazy town
this servingman or clown
will not believe the play's on fire
but still puts out smudged wits for hire
skipping and dancing here and there
                      here and there
to answer any ghost that calls
for something to wet his whistle, faintly, impossibly calls.

Here is a stage where only
a fool would have the heart
to play this fellow's part
running to get his fingers burnt
then showing some new step he's learnt
bewildered but still grinning
                     and spinning round and round
one bright patch left in the smoke
now the principals are leaving, with all prudent folk.

Yes, a common pitiful thing.
But children who find him delight-
ful may still after all be right.
For they saw him on the stage alone

182

take a bird from his white breast-bone
and loose it into the flames.
                              And it flew swiftly on
till before a tongue could speak
it coasted back to his lips with a cherry-red song in its beak.

The sky as apple
cut open and shining pale-green in the early evening
innocence and experience both.

The sky as melon
streaked with white clouds widening gradually toward the zenith
voluptuousness of midnight.

Or frosted, tufted
with seeds of blood-red pomegranate edged with white
iced there in delirium

till the moment passes
and the sky fulfils itself in a turbulent rush of crimson
to death and dark.

Or in another zone
another hemisphere where day after day
sky builds its flawless empires

over towers building
and unbuilding, creation and destruction
their weaving and unweaving,

light clinging there as peach,
as flesh, compassionate, around the seamed scarred earth
whose fosses run with blood.

Compassionate topaze, turquoise –
or sky as delicate as a sea-blue mist of unicorns
and orreries

when in this
hemisphere the sun stands frozen at the summer solstice
and everything seems possible.

So many skies!
so many worlds, so many modes of life and consciousness,
such blue infinitudes!

Once as a boy
while lying on warm rock I drank the sky brim-full
and dreamed, dreamed

with eyes made pure and deep
while overhead one pale white cloud disposed itself
to blessedness.

Now fifty years have gone
but, strange! the same dream lasts, that that same cloud or angel
may lead us on.

The effect of bronze and the effect of water,
that is what my art would capture.

Bronze rivered by the weather and the rain
and water sinewy and muscular.

All male, the sea writhes like a serpent,
runs green and rippling through its hellespont.

Prowess of wind-veins, shifting water-hues
mirrors the water of a bronze cuirass.

Lashed to a froth, the armed and armoured sea
can crush whole armies. Valour of bronze
is forged from salt inconstancy,
veined with the sea's sway, riddled with sea-myths.

On a warrior battling with the waves
a warrior battling with himself
light wavers. Sword-play in sunlight. Deep eclipse.
Splendour again. Star-showers of spray!

Water and bronze, bronze and water,
two currents making for a single ocean,

two mirrors melting, two rivers meeting —
that broad deep gulf, a man.

The ground that the figure rises from
involves wolves and wild strawberries.

His hair is as black as the hull of a schooner.
His eye takes in oceans and provinces.

He's deep down a mine, and crucified
on the glaciers. He's wind, he's sun,

and a dark cloud bringing snow over Labrador,
and the taut light over the tundra.

He holds the statistical series in one hand
and they begin to sprout. They swell like grain.

He moves like a spy through the constitution
till it gives up its secrets. Even the slums

and the negroes can feel the difference
now this calm voice is come to judgement.

A spar-tree in a thick rain-forest,
a stand of spruce, a black spruce swamp,

where a white-throat trails its one sweet note
shyly, secretly. So shy and secret . . .

but his feet draw up the blood of the young men
who died at the rapids defending the city

and of the Indians too who died in the attack
and of the French and English who died on the heights.

That blood comes into his mouth — salt,
as he swathes through the bush for a new hydro-line

or runs to shoulder the weight when the damp pulp
breaks or the paper is fluttering like sails.

Where was he last seen? At an airport
on the prairies, the sky high and handsome,

or dropping down at dusk with engines idling
to a gulf of moss-green, grape-blue soundings

that deepen and widen past the straits
out into the ribs and vaults of ocean.

Space enters his bloodstream. He races the sun
from one end of the country to the other.

And yet is still, still. In the end rock,
rock and a habitation on the rock

where roses were planted generations ago
and left untended, a wild sweet land,

ground of our defeats and disappointments, ours,
that still in this figure may break in flower.

SONG FOR A SOLDIER'S GUITAR

(for the Jack whom I served with in Italy, 1944—45)

As I shuffle and cut to coax something back
The cards are all faceless, greasy the pack,
Till out from the rest there flutters a Jack.
There's spring in his step and storm on his track,
    This Jack of diamonds, of diamonds.

A knave — well, not really — but dangerous in drink
To bust in a face and land in the clink.
He's sweet with his fists and lithe as a mink
And would far rather fight than be troubled to think.

Jack lackland, and learning, but never lacklustre.
His side-arms were shiny, he was smart on a muster.
In action his mess-mates around him would cluster
As though his bare hands were a match for disaster.

Time, I suppose, will surely betray
Him, and carry his luck and his lustre away.
Well, he will make good whatever's to pay
With mettle too precious for time to assay.

Perhaps he is guilty of heretic pride,
By averages outlawed, by the prudent denied.
Then prudence be damned! It's with him I'd be tried,
With a world to outface, but this Jack by my side,
    This Jack of diamonds, of diamonds.

VICTORY

(after the statue by Michelangelo in the Palazzo Vecchio)

You can see how much love has gone into the modelling of the
　　　young man's flanks
untouchable!
and the young man's eye so blank and sovereign
absorbing the world.
But how strong too the old man's head between the hero's feet
bowed, bent, but still unvanquished.
So a god might shoulder a world
and be full of longing.
And which is more terrible,
the young man's eye or the power and knowledge in the old
　　　man's shoulders?

LAMENT FOR MARSYAS

Tall as a spar
        and black as a spar
A black spar that the wind peels and whips
Till it ripples in stripling strength, yet rooted
In stillness
      in the deep
           suck of the sea.

Why does that distant image haunt me so?
I knew him, true, but then we went our different ways
He to his fate and I to place and fortune.
Under the god's bright visage we others would
Sit deliberating new statutes, tributes,
New colonies to be established by
The orderly diffusion of hallowed fire.
He would be out wandering on the lawless roads
Or, returned at night-fall from the hill-sides or the sea,
Would haunt the fish-wharfs and the leafy wine-shops.
Sometimes his arms were bright with fish-scales, silvery,
He might have been a merman in the moon
But then a cloud would pass and he grew green and leafy.
He had his own companions, a ragged crew,
And there were stories told of all-night orgies
Of how he stained the day-break reeling home,
His temples flushed, his cheeks bruised blue as grape-skins,
His tunic torn and wet with sweat, his black hair dripping.
They may be true, the stories that were told,
But mostly when I saw him he would be alone.
One evening late I saw him sitting by himself,
Lord of an empty tavern, with only a candle breathing by his side
And gazing at the half-empty wine-cup in his hand
As though he had been chosen in a way he could not understand.

A tall spar
        a tall spar in a broken boat.
My bowels were strangely loosened.

What is the dark pool mounting in my loins,
A dark pool mounting, quivering? In dark complicity
I felt that shuddering again the day he died.
A great cloud of light and in the brightness a black
Spar foundering. I did not want to see it.
A black spar tossing, foundering. A black
Head bowed and broken. His agony was mine, mine.
I did not want to see it. Light. Ambush of sharp spring light.
Light like a knife-edge. Feet hurrying towards a flute.
And through the light the god advancing,
His stronger music flowing like his tunic folds,
His curls are majesty and music both,
Perfection tangles there to triumph over the rude flute,
Over the stripped savage limbs, to triumph everywhere.
The very air draws blood. I do not want to see it.
Their gazes meeting as though they were two mortals,
Marsyas wounded by Apollo's brightness
And Apollo wounded by the outlaw's love,
Their gazes meeting, melting, in one wide wound.
But now my eyes are shut. And when they open
All that is left is Marsyas hanging from a pine-tree.

A black spar broken
                  peeled and whipped by the wind
By lightning splintered, by the dayspring shattered
And scattered far and wide, to the four winds drifting,
But then given back
              from sea
                  suck
                      to the forests and the hills.

I have done everything that a man can do,
Or so I thought, seen, suffered everything.
But that great cry of love before he died
To god the dayspring who was ruining him
Came from a world beyond me. I shut my ears
But it comes back and back, his voice piercing me
As I am sacrificing, at home or on campaigns,
Or exercising, or in the market-place,
His dead body calling to me, whispering to me,
As I lie muffled in my cloak with longing.
I have given my love to many in my time
To the mother of my children, to others who
Were nameless, to one dearer than all the rest.
But only with his death the knife-edge of beauty,
The terror in the beauty that we love, and must love,
And what's in us forever unappeasable
Calls me to wisdom in a world unknown.
Only now I know that Apollo's curls and Marsyas'
Shaggy thighs are twined in furious union.
Only now I know they both still live in me
To be offered to the glory of the light
And to the glory of the funeral pyre.
Before, as I would turn his exile in my hand
In fear and exultation and contempt, I thought
Of him as outcast only, like ordure in the streets.
Now I believe him part of the colouring of day.

WILDMAN CAROL

Our saviour was a wildman
  And was born among the beasts.
So bring boughs of sacred wildness
  To celebrate his feasts.

God, man, and animal,
  He haunts the wilderness
Where libertines and outlaws
  Come to him to confess.

Confess their serpent darkness,
  Their coils of heavenly guilt,
Confess the pools of blood
  Their savagery has spilt.

How shall the earth be quickened
  Except by savage blood?
How shall the earth be ransomed
  If savagery be good?

His shaggy brow is hidden
  In curls of youthfulness
His shaggy thighs run purple
  With the godhead of distress.

God, man, and animal,
  His lot is to be slain
And then from lustrous greenery
  In strength to rise again.

His strength is miracle,
  His fresh green wound the Word,
"Do unto others," the soft cry
  The wilderness has heard.

And animal creation
  Acclaims a paradox.
The wildman from the woods,
  He breeds the gentlest flocks —

Gentle and savage both,
  The noblest of our kind.
So green boughs bring for feasting,
  The freshest you can find.

Stove in, the flesh he was travelling in, his face
punched full of figures. A fluke from leviathan
caught him and he capsized, down down
in a dry death. Accountants searching
his failure with rubber-gloved hands drew out
a typical balance-sheet of delicate red frustrations,
a whole corporation of losses.

So far nothing so very unusual, nothing
that couldn't be cured by a simple proceeding in bankruptcy,
the creditors paid off at ten cents on the dollar, with nobody
else any the wiser (after all
the streets are full of the dead, the disfigured, and the walking
        wounded).
But this casualty wouldn't behave as though nothing had
        happened,
kept calling for his mother, made water in the streets, and cried
        and cried,
and wouldn't be comforted even when they told him
of all the ten-lane highways they were building for him
and the shopping plazas and the new planetarium.
Clearly that couldn't go on. Not when
raccoons began infesting the city
and a deer blundered one morning into the stock-exchange.
There was even a rumour that a unicorn had been seen in the
        suburbs.
In secret session the city fathers declared him officially dead,
and authorized the coroners to conduct an autopsy,
and investigate, and report, with full powers
under the Public Enquiries Act.
When they picked him up he was standing at a street-corner
singing "Love, I laid my love away" — a song of his own
that sounded a little like "Careless Love," only slower and sadder
as he sung it with tears streaming down

as though he were mourning for a boat stove in and drifting
away, lost love, lost hope, with tissues unravelling into the gutter.
He came quietly, and answered their questions as well as he could.
How had it all begun? He couldn't remember exactly,
but he had always been good at games. . . . What could that
have to do with it? Well, the guidance teacher
suggested he might go on into games theory and linear
           programming,
and before long he was in charge of a whole room of key-punch
           operators.
Soon he moved over to Acetates Unlimited to run
their sampling and forecasting. He had been getting along
           famously, then,
whatever happened? His big break came (this said with a sigh, a
           deep sigh)
when he was appointed to Defence Research as head
           econometrist.
"You had it made. Come, what was it happened?"
"One morning I was examining one of the models when
a variable shifted and I fell, it must have been thirty feet.
I felt as though I'd broken my back.
Sometimes I think I'd be better off dead."

He didn't whimper when they sliced back his muscles
and cut open his gut and took out the organs.
But when they reached for his sex he screamed like a bird,
his flesh switched to scrap, his nerves wires, his eyes
deflowered through the sockets of his skull
till they flowered again in immaculate spirals of copper foil,
his spine coiled with rust-proof tubing.
And he slid from the mortuary-slab
and strode invulnerably away.

Clanking a little as he went, he moved through
the market with exemplary candour
offering for sale skeins of perfectly machined ball-bearings

and nickel-alloy prospects sprouting from his shoulders.
No takers, though.
                    But now he has found his niche.
A businessman of imagination has seen his possibilities
and bought him lock stock and barrel
to hang (as a warning? as a guide to the future?)
over the door of the aluminum company's new extrusion plant.

SELF-PORTRAIT AS STRAWMAN

The grasses blow on the rock
and I blow with them.
I sigh as the winds sigh,
this way and that, my feet on the rock
my back crutched on scrub-oak, jack-pine and poplar
my head thatched with grasses, with sweet grasses, plaited
that trail down shading my eyes.
My eyes so dote on the light in the chokecherries till, delighted,
they take them for pupils, I need no sight of my own.
My wife is turned from me, my sons are away.
But who am I? and where? and what have I done?
Those questions are sighed away on the wind, are like straw.
The coteries of the birds accept me.

The warblers come to my hand,
they warp round my shoulders.
I am no more alien than the leaves
or the air they so mollify
with suave plumage, dove-grey or olive or green.
Have I fallen? I don't know. My feet are on rock.
My wits search down into my flesh, drowsily,
are washed clear by lymphs in their endless streams
that, circling, build up a whole world with its own
myth of creation, regeneration and decay —
that will last at least for a day. For a day? My right
here is as great as the grasshoppers'
or the chipmunks' chattering chattering as they pillage the acorns.

Still blow the grasses
and I blow with them,
this way and that, in shadow and sun
on rock that is older than time.
Rock, moss, lichen, and lichen over the moss,
give me grounds for staring quartz in the eye,

and feldspar, and mica, and boulder-beds teetering on granite,
ice-ages forgotten at last and glaciers,
and my own full share of fury and fire
and the still longer agony of agony cooling
till now
like the harebells that blow at my feet
or ground-cranberries trailing from fissures of rock,
I sigh with the winds and the grasses, unbroken.

WHILING AWAY AN AUGUST AFTERNOON

After reading the latest news about stocks of nuclear warheads
I put down the paper and stroll over towards the beach
and stand in the shade of young poplars.
As I touch the cool bark
a pale grey-green dust comes off on my hand.

I hadn't believed I could still do anything so innocent.
But then I remember that few things are so self-delighting
as a young sapling, so perfectly androgynous,
so like unfallen Adam
as God created him and the learned rabbis vouch for.

Even so, a small darker patch remains where my hand for a
        moment rested.

In the distance
        a red and white canister
                perhaps a little tilted,
balanced precariously on red granite, miles from shore.

Land there on a calm day (and you can't land on any other day)
and you will admire the stone walls, coated in steel, seven feet
        through at the base,
and the sheer audacity of having put a lighthouse there
with hardly enough room for a helicopter landing-pad.
Then, while admiring the interior economy, climb up three floors
to the light at the top and come out to gaze sixty feet down
at the sea's pelt rippling silkily over the shoals
in an August heat-haze, the sun teeming and swaying.
It is marvellous, you say, as you look back and leave it.

But it's a marvel that may not leave *you* — to return as a vision
in different weather, the seas leaping over the light, black and
        green
and slippery as a whale. I sit there cowering and exultant
in a November gale, sitting in the belly of a whale
as though leviathan had reared up on its tail.
Black night, black cloud, black water hide me
as I go about and do the petty chores, listening to the generator,
feeling faintly sick with the smell of diesel-oil,
proud of the radium-vapour light that never can go out
(though that's due more to God than me)
circumferenced everywhere by the horizon when the seas will
        let it.
I feel as pent as Jonah and as trembling as a boy
my precious past reduced to fear and trembling
as I put the head-set on and hear another world come trickling in.
And yet I hardly care, that other world's so far away,

wife, children, wars and rumours, and the millions fallen at
        my side,
and all I've done and all I've failed to do
even the fact that I can say, I've tried, I've tried,
all the stale failures lying on my plate
and all the triumphs where I set my pride
are shrunken here or vanished.
I make my bed and make my peace in this leviathan
that rears up wild and lashing on its tail.
I am alone with some few of the lonely lovely dead
and try to make my peace with this close air
where the thought of dying trickles everywhere
and pray
        I may wake singing when the storm is over
           "Lo, the bright seraphim"
and be released and whirled up lightly as a bird
to see the dayspring, and God glorified.

A RADIANCE

(in memory of my sister, Elizabeth Josephine)

How you still shine!

I see you
sitting on the dock to dry your hair.
A canoe of mandarin red in the hot sun blazing.
Towels. Paddles varnished and gleaming like fish scales.
As mink play on the rock, and I swim lazily on my back
and (moving in and out of the scene) look back
at the mink, and the canoe, and the paddles, and a birch-tree
white and green under the clear blue sky, and you under the
       birch-tree.
And when I climb out on the dock a few minutes later
and ask about a bruise on your arm
all you say, easily, lightly, is, "I bruise easily."

(You are what I can never be forgiven,
stronger than I, more easily broken.)

I see you
(now I am seas and continents away)
paddling alone far out in the open
of our broad sweet-water sea, the waves gentled
by the summer sun, and silky, sea-green
over the undulant shoals, farther and farther out,
(so you said later), with the thought beginning
to form of not returning, the canoe lapsing and lisping
over the gentled waves, you guiding its light sweet will

with your strong sweet will, not knowing yet what it was
or where it would carry you. But returning at last
through the shoals
while you still could make out the beacons.

(I the only one who could have saved you,
I failed you.)

I see you,
your absence in the rooms you made your own,
fresh, cool, immaculate, like lily-of-the-valley,
a spectrum now blended into perfect whiteness,
untainted by the tell-tale streaks and stains of madness
as I sit down to take an inventory —
an inventory of pain and loss and absence.
In the winter sun, straw-coloured matting.
Grey walls. A polished walnut table.
Your records,
the unplayed music rising, blending, into silence,
everything left as you would have it left,
and a deafening silence round the boxes of my letters that you
         kept.
(Even our handwriting was the same,
my hand that could have saved you.)

Now my eyes close
or almost.
My pupils close to pinpricks.
The rooms drift up with snow.

I see you in the snow,
great February drifts where you had walked alone,
snow white as morphine, merciless,
great billows of it where you were drowned, your hands
and feet sucked under, mortified, white sheets
drawn level with your sunken eyes, clouds

that fell on you, on your eyes, your lustrous hair.
Is there some realm of mercy in the clouds?
some hands into whose mercy I might yield you up?
some realm where I might be forgiven?

So we are told. And so I falteringly believe.
For as I falter on I see you shining still,
death's matchless bride
still radiant,
radiant beneath a canopy of swords.

We have cut down a tree, my brother and I,
an old dead tree, some thirty feet high,
that, falling, gulped out brown velvet rot
great mouthfuls of it that both of us thought
was as dead as anything well could be
once struck by lightning and then utterly
honeycombed, hived, to ripe decay
by woodpeckers needling it day after day.
But no, not quite. There are two baby flickers
there on the ground, with bright red stickers
to know them by on the backs of their necks,
cheeping a little from their infant beaks,
their eyes tight shut, still almost asleep
in their honey-gold down, a dream as deep
as when they were cradled up there in their nest.
That was years ago when the light was best.
But, God, since then how the rot has spread!
rot in my eyes, rot in my head.
It was Swift who said he would die like that tree,
he would die at the top. So it may prove with me.
Yet if that is so, but still lasts some light
where a man may turn who's been struck by blight
could anything be better than at last to shake
gold fledglings down for the morning's sake?

THE BEAVER

Sober, industrious, a good husband and father,
spending his life in capital formation and domestic bliss.
He had been cutting his teeth on the capitalist ethic
long before the pale-face entrepreneurs caught up with him —
and skinned him, of course.

Still there is something a little mysterious about this good
            bourgeois.
When he slaps his tail on the water of an evening
and disappears, where does he go
before he reappears so sleek and glistening?

That's something I can't answer.
But the early travellers reported the tail is delicious.

THE MOOSE, OR MODES OF PERCEPTION

Moosehead, moosehide, moosemeat —
but there are other ways of looking at a moose
than simply as an object to kill and dismember.

I suppose the best way is to come on it at a turn of the river
as you're paddling downstream and see it as big as a horse
with a great hump at its shoulders to support its head and its antlers
but with spindly ungainly legs that splash through the shallows
as it gallops away into the bush. That's how my sons
see it, they tell me, in the rivers north of Superior.
That way you can share in its primal native existence.

Another way belongs to the historian or pre-
historian, who will tell you it was one of the first pathfinders
even before the Indians or the *coureurs de bois,*
the first to trample the portages around the rapids
before there were canoes to carry, or packs, or muskets.
The evidence might seem perhaps a little flimsy
but that is the verdict of those who most ought to know.

Or look at it sexually. Like most other mammals than man
it has a bone in its penis, which should make for ready
performance and lessen the need for sex aids and manuals.
It differs also in this, that it only ruts in the fall.
But then what a wing-ding! Sometimes two bulls
in their fight for possession get their antlers so locked
that they can't get them disentangled, and founder, and die.

("Make love not war," you say. The slogan sounds good.
But, man! you ought to know the two are not antithetical.)

Then there is the mode of contemplation. If you stay
down-wind and hidden, you can sometimes watch a moose
for hours quietly browsing the twigs from young poplars

or standing in shallow water, its great head down,
and the long stem of a water-lily trailing from its mouth.
That still mode has advantages for looking at a creature
that is usually so solitary, so shy and withdrawn.

In any case, believe me, there is more to a moose
than what is left after it is killed and dismembered
more than
moosehead, moosehide, moosemeat.

It suggests we could have our own kind of ecstasy
if we would. At least it doesn't exist in Europe,
this tiny heart that keeps the wings so furiously beating
till time stands still, in a transparency,
a clot of deeper light on the sunlight over the rock
rose trellised on a stem of air.

Sun, sweetness, savagery
distilled into a drop from the rainbow's edge
a promise of love and freedom that the heart drinks up
and, losing it, grieves
as it darts away and is lost in the light through the pine-trees.

But stand in the clearing and wait. Again
a deep kiss from nowhere can pierce the savagely trembling
          silence.

A pale green sky to the north
and under it islands with pines that now are the colour of
       lamp-black
and one song as night deepens (the only song for a long time now)
that is more a threat or a plea than a song, a hoarse lover's plea,
"Whip-poor-will, whip-poor-will, whip-poor-will,"
and so on and on endlessly to exhaustion or consummation
till night is complete and all the islands are mainland.

This is the new world's nightingale
as hidden, as secret, as deeply nocturnal,
incessantly exploring the ground between love and pain
but with three notes only instead of orchestral richness.
One mild spring night in a garden in Suffolk
I was spangled by surprise with the notes of the nightingale
as though a whole baroque consort had been set up in the garden
to drench me in diamonds. But now when I think of love and pain
I hear only those three taut notes from a cold green sky.

In Persia the nightingale sang for love of the rose
and flew on in lyric verse across Arabia
and along the shores of North Africa on into Spain and Provence
singing of the pain of love unsatisfied,
and of the beauty of love, and of the pain in the beauty of love,
with many arabesques, but always with something courtly
as well as something blood-red and carnal about each of them.

But there are no arabesques to our nightingale
as it sings from the green northern sky with its wide dark mouth,
"Whip-poor-will, whip-poor-will, whip-poor-will."
This is the frank desire of love to hurt, to give pain,
a part of the sado-masochistic covering around normal sex
(whatever that is!)
a part of the love that loves to be partnered with pain.

IN PRAISE OF PORCUPINES

They have a kind of sour waxy smell that most humans don't
      fancy.
But the antipathy isn't reciprocal.
Everything we touch, to them is simply divine,
especially everything to do with a house or an outhouse
where they can gnaw away happily night after night.

Clearly not a creature of the most delicate tastes.
But don't be too quick to despise or, above all,
to believe that old story about their being so easy to kill.
Get one of them up a tree and you'll soon see how hard it is to get
      him down.
Even direct hits seem to bounce off his quills.

The moral, I suppose, is that you can have known the worst
      human stenches
and still want to live.

THE BEAVER: MARK II

According to Leonardo, who should have known
(being the wisest man of his age
or perhaps of any other age),
the beaver
"when it is pursued
bites off its testicles with its sharp teeth
and leaves them to its enemies."

A neat trick if you can do it.
But I offer it to you for what it is worth.
It has helped me a little to understand
the behaviour of some of our more gutless wonders.

THE OSPREY, OR HOW ANIMALS ARE NAMED

We were sitting after supper in the cabin
with all the windows open as a hot still day
simmered down to a still and beautiful clarity.
When suddenly a great pair of wings swept down
and shut out the light and plucked something out of the water
and was up and away before we could get to our feet.
"What was it?" we asked one another once a slight tremor
of fear was over. It couldn't be a heron. Or a hawk.
It was too large, we thought, to have been an eagle. So,
since we didn't know what it was, we called it an osprey.

Sweet-mouth, honey-paws, hairy one!
you don't prowl much in the history books
but you sure figure when choker-men, donkey-men, shanty-men
        gather,
or pulp-savages, or top-riggers.
"I've seen me go up a tree so fast with one of them after me
I only had time to loosen my belt and give him my pants
or I'd have been done for."
"When I came into the cook-house I knew there was something
        there.
And was there ever! A great big black bear.
He chased me round and round the table till I hauled off and hit
        the dinner gong.
That shook him! He was out the door like a bat out of hell."
If only you could hear us talk, you would know how we love you
sweet-mouth, honey-paws, hairy one!

Cousin, comrade, and jester,
so like us as you pad along jocularly
looking for garbage and honey, and not leaving much trace,
dozing off (for a whole season — as who wouldn't want to?)
then when you waken, perhaps a little too devil-may-care,
not knowing your own strength, ready to carry a joke a little too far,
creature of moods, old man, young man, child,
sitting in a meadow eating blueberries by the bushful.

Don't you know how much we love you?
Old man, curled up in your lair? So come out and be killed, old
        man!
Sweet-mouth, honey-paws, hairy one!

A ROUGH SWEET LAND

I

Air without angels, sky without sound.

The great sway of cloudless splendour, that draws profound
sweetness from the water and the sun, swirls
with a trillion scintillations, light scattering light,
light washing waves, light breaking into particles
(but still waves), still towering to meridian stillness
from the bare backs of the paddlers resting — and the varnished
blades on the varnished gunwales — up to the uninflected
zenith through an atmosphere set free from accidence,
a great tower of light now, now trembling in time without tense.

If there were angels
they would hold in their reconciling eyes . . .

a whole wild dialectic of lakes and rivers
one wide resolution leading to another tension
water wide-eyed in the sun, in glittering contemplation
then passionate, strained, dark-lidded, flumed through
rock, till the canoe is catapulted out in a froth
of eddying foam (their flesh whipped too to froth)
down a wind-whipped lake where interlacing birch
and spruce lattice the lusts of animals coupling and killing.
Angels alone would see it whole and one — complete
cantata — broad basin brimmed with animal heat,
great shaggy animal head half-drenched half-drowned
in intricate bright perplexities.
No angels, though, there are none. A distant
helicopter hovers. An eagle screams from a clear sky.
No angels. . . . Except for this cloudless moment
when the sun, solvent of categories, stands sole and sovereign,
process runs on. The canoeists wonder if they

have taken the right fork or what lies beyond another bend.
Solutions lead to other problems.

And farther north
forest giving out to tundra (like matter giving out to number)
mind giving out, barren-lands, snow, ice,
whole archipelagos of it.

Through the mist
bows lisping the current, bright bows of weathered birch-bark
patched with spruce-gum, vermilion paddles flashing
as a brigade of *canots du nord* drives upstream
to make Fort Chipewyan before the freeze-up.
And the bourgeois in his counting-house in Montreal
imposes his will with paper promises and the paddlers' shoulders
on a future where his arteries will turn to steel
his vanities to a wilderness of markets.
The sun stands still. Two hundred years are nothing, nothing.
Storms melt into sunshine, wreck into valiant splendour.
Squalls, downpours, hardships, are licked to sweetness
by a moody tyrant a hundred million miles away
whose tongue lolls out to upset ages, climates,
species, and set continents adrift, hinting
that there is something still to find in all this welter.
Faults and fissures, glacial scourings, sand. And on
the sandbar footprints of other animals, firm pad
of a great black bear come out of the woods to fish,
the delicate track of mink, skimmings of sea-birds, sand-birds,
at the water's edge, all signatures of possibilities
that the sunlight's power defines impartially.
Light falls, and hangs, and sways, shimmering with possibilities
mirroring violence, mirroring pain,
mirroring a state where mind undoes the damage it has done,
where the body heals itself, mind heals itself
as light towers timelessly, showering with all occasions.

And shimmering by the rapids
are yards of sodden trade-goods drying in the sun.

II

Air without angels, sky without sound.

But sometimes
in the deep heat of an August afternoon
the land opens, offers itself.
Stillness. The pines give up their resin to
the heat. Warblers are nesting. Stillness.
Not a flicker of a breeze among the poplars,
the cardinal flowers hang heavy. Stillness.
But balm, a breath of balsam, healing. The land
gives out the savour of a risen body,
stirs with the presence of a naked body
that lives and fills the air like balsam.
Voluptuous the heat and light as he begins
to move voluptuously, as sweet as honey, the colour
of honey, deeper than that, deep honey-gold and brown,
sweetness emerging from the rock of strength.

He moves and godhead gathers, light gathers
clustering his hair with brightness, darkness, the colour
of light-blue, dark-blue grapes, the sheen of grapes,
his breast is cuirassed with light, moulded
and modelled ripplingly his naked torso,
his flanks a bloom of strenuous freshness
that spills and scatters as he moves, moves
on the tindery needles and parched moss, the thirst
of summer at its towering height, when
air is full of sudden short-lived luxury —
lush raspberry-red of sumach's candelabra,
beds of wild raspberries, wild roses blooming,
rich cardinal-flowers in shadow. And shadowed too
the source of his strength, the source of the tenderness
that floods his slow unfolding hands like flowers
is hidden in deep violet shadow. Air rich
but wafer-thin and rippling. A steady pulse...

of air athrob with godhead and deep placid lust,
exhaling glorias of animal heat,
as turning he seems to summon a movement of dancers.

Where has he come from
this grave dancer in the heat,
whose movements all are stillness
of turning shoulders, waist, and ankles,
moving to his own measure, his own grave measure
in sun, in shade?

This body stark as an Indian's, and as tawny,
this warrior's grace — perhaps arising from a time
before the white man came? when young braves
danced their war-dance and went on hunting-parties
for deer and bear and still that best prize, man.
Where is his war-paint, then, and sorcery, and treachery?
No, his eyes gaze into clearer skies.
Or it may be that he came like Dionysus sailing,
fluted, with grapes and vine-leaves, from the far Aegean;
through fertile Tuscany, of hill-side vineyards
and cypresses and pine-trees, whose landscape melts
into the sweet fictions of perspective
its masters first explored in lyrical researches;
through Aquitaine, of vintages and castles,
and other provinces abundant in enclosures,
where fountains play to the admiration of pools,
and espaliered pears are ripening.
                                        But no,
his is a new treaty with a new environment,
his eyeballs catch the glint of ice in August
as ours do. And he is new now, new and ours, and always.

III

Air without angels, sky without sound.

The great sway of new felicity that swirls round
his naked shoulders is god answering god, light answering
light, light scattering light but still light.
New hymns, new poles, new possibilities
arrowing into the soundless towering atmosphere
from where his gaze is orbed in tension and resolution
both, a great bow bent − suffering and repression tensed
to triumph − a gaze both wounded and unwounded,
a great bow bent in his human heavy-lidded eyes
made from the forest of perplexities.

But streams run on
past splendour, solstice, sandbars, rapids, chutes.

Streams running on
to storms, frustrations, loss.

Streams running on
in new researches, lyrical researches.

Streams running on . . .

to cities with greed and compound interest clotted
under a leaden halo steaming simmering
where the entrepreneurs cry "More! More!" turning the heat
up till the mercury bursts in the mouth and poisons the patient,
where highways are hernias, and sirens are screaming like crazy
through sunless labyrinths to wan endless wards
or reeking kitchens for immediate surgery of a leg,
or an arm, or a lung, the fever-charts hectic,
cheeks bloated with cancer, lips pleading for numbness or death.
(And other cities longing to discharge their paranoia
in flights of many-headed birds so shrewdly

programmed for their prey – which is life, all life.)
Only the hovels are human, and only the hucksters are happy.
The others can find their peace where they can, in drugs
or under the wheels of the subways, in diving from bridges
or in the heavy stupor after shock and largactil,
while in broad day the whip-poor-will calls and calls for the mercy
      of night.

But streams run on
past long portages, hard portages, to other streams
with new explorers, new voyageurs.

Streams running on
into the arms of love (I am travelling new streams,
I am travelling blindfold into your arms, I am writing
this poem for you).

Streams running on
under grave eyes that have seen and suffered everything
and know that there is something still to find.

Streams running on
into a presence that has moved past need and honour
to delight, beckoning to islands where
the winds blow soft, where the trees all smell of honey.

Streams running on...

to cities that still bear the freshness of discovery,
swept by a paddler's breeze and washed continually
by searches and researches for something still to find
through labyrinths (where sometimes love makes limits),
for a paradise that's still to find, through prospects
of a muffled suffering city where nature welters
with so many possibilities – of mountebanks
and clowns and harlequins and vaguely drifting
vaguely disaffected crowds – where power is present,
but another presence too that overrules the rulers.

A god-like dancer bringing balm and healing
is moving secretly as on an August afternoon
till — is it a vision only? — the heavens sometimes open
and a great sway of cloudless splendour, that draws profound
sweetness from the water and the sun, swirls
with a trillion scintillations, light scattering light,
light washing waves, light breaking into particles
(but still waves), still towering to meridian stillness
above this most improbable but blessed ground
in air without angels, sky without sound.

NOTES

This volume reprints the whole of *The Wounded Prince* (1948), *The Net and the Sword* (1953), and *Something Still to Find* (1982). "One of the Regiment," which originally appeared in *The Wounded Prince* and was reprinted in *The Net and the Sword*, appears here with the poems of the later volume.

WEATHERING IT

page 13 The drowsiness of Kutúzov is drawn from Tolstoy's account in *War and Peace* of the campaign that culminated in Napoleon's victory at Austerlitz in 1805 over the combined armies of Russia and Austria.

page 15 The Polish Army Camp at Niagara-on-the-Lake from 1917 to 1919 trained Polish volunteers who served overseas as two divisions in the French army. The camp was in Canada and was staffed by Canadian officers; the bills were met by the French government. The volunteers were Poles, most of whom spoke only Polish and who came almost entirely from the United States – and with the blessing of the United States government.

page 21 "Romanza" rather than "romance," in order to suggest the musical, rather than the literary, associations of the word. If the reader is reminded of the romanza, the marvellous second movement, of Mozart's piano concerto in D-minor (K.466), so much the better.

page 28 The detail about Mrs. Simcoe and the rattlesnakes comes from the diary which she kept during her stay in Canada from 1791 to 1796, while her husband was the first Lieutenant-Governor of Upper Canada, now Ontario.

page 35 Before the final successful attack on Cassino in May 1944, there had been several unsuccessful, and very costly, attacks – the first by the United States Fifth Army in January 1944 and another by the Second New Zealand Corps in the following month.

page 45   Duncan Phillips founded the Phillips Gallery in Washington, D.C., one of the most pleasurable and distinguished small galleries in the world.

page 50   Mozart was thirteen, almost fourteen, when this portrait of him was painted in Verona in January 1770. The artist is believed to have been Saverio dalla Rosa.

page 56   See the illustrations to the *De Humani Corporis Fabrica* by Vesalius, published in 1543.

page 60   The battle for Ortona in December 1943 was one of the bloodiest in which soldiers of the Canadian army engaged during the Second World War.

SOMETHING STILL TO FIND

page 156   Etienne Brulé was one of Champlain's *"jeunes garçons,"* whom he used as guides and interpreters after he had sent them to live with the Indians. Brulé is believed to have been the first white man to see four of the Great Lakes — Lake Huron, Lake Ontario, Lake Erie and Lake Superior. Ultimately, in 1633, he was killed and eaten by the Hurons among whom he was living.

page 167   In the fall of 1609, when Champlain on returning from his first voyage to New France was received in audience at Fontainebleau by Henri IV, he presented the King with a belt of porcupine quills and two scarlet tanagers.

page 173   An astrolabe, believed to be Champlain's, was found in 1867 on the canoe-route between the Ottawa River and Georgian Bay. It is now in the collection of the New York Historical Society.

page 179   The wild orchid *Cypripedium acaule* is popularly called either moccasin plant or lady slipper.

page 194   For Christ imagined and presented as an *homo silvaticus*, or sylvan man, see Roberto Longhi, *Piero della Francesca*, pp. 33–34 and pp. 89–91.

page 202   Red Rock Light is the principal navigation aid on the channel leading in from Georgian Bay to Parry Sound.

page 208   For beavers' tails as a delicacy, see Harold A. Innis, *The Fur Trade in Canada*, p. 2.

INDEX OF TITLES